The Road Washes Out in Spring

The Road Washes Out in Spring

A POET'S MEMOIR OF LIVING OFF THE GRID

Baron Wormser

University Press of New England
Hanover and London

Published by University Press of New England,

One Court Street, Lebanon, NH 03766

www.upne.com

First University Press of New England paperback edition 2008

Printed in the United States of America

5 4 3 2 1

ISBNs for the paperback edition:

ISBN-13: 978-1-58465-704-0

ISBN-10: 1-58465-704-9

CIP data appear at the end of the book

This book does not purport to be an annal. As memory is subjective and partial, it has a fictive aspect. Names have been changed accordingly.

Acknowledgments

Special thanks to Christopher Holt and Nina Ryan.

Grateful acknowledgment is made to the editors and publishers of the following journals in which excerpts of this book first appeared: *Agni Magazine, The Fourth River,* and *Accent.* "Building a House in the Woods, Maine, 1971" first appeared in *Contemporary Poetry of New England.* It was read at the inauguration of Governor John Baldacci in January 2003.

Quotes from "The Hill Wife," "The Need of Being Versed in Country Things," "Birches," and "Good-By and Keep Cold" from *The Poetry of Robert Frost* edited by Edward Connery Lathem. Copyright 1916, 1923, 1969 by Henry

(Continued on page 200)

University Press of New England is a member of the Green Press Initiative. The paper used in this book meets their minimum requirement for recycled paper.

For Janet, Maisie, and Owen

The Road Washes Out in Spring

Building a House in the Woods, Maine, 1971

A good uphill mile and a half from a not very good
                                       dirt road,
That distance on foot meaning a sort of mincing strut
                                   over frost heaves
And washouts across what had been a poor road at best
                                   fifty years previously,
Through tangles of witch hazel, alder and birch saplings
                                 and—at this time
Of year in the low spots—sucking gurgling mud:
                                 that expedition
Taking the better part of an hour to a ridge side where
                                 a few gaunt, disheartened
Apple trees and dead elms from the nineteenth century
                                 stood like blank-eyed
Sentinels and where you intended to build a house
                                 that would stare
Without curtains at a prospect of more ridges and then
                                 real mountains that
Receded to the serene distance of pale green eternity.

And why shouldn't love be made here, meals cooked and
                                 consumed, fires stoked,
Children born who would have the boundless woods to learn from,
                                 who would feel freedom
In their footsteps and taste the calm thrill of dawn.
                                 Weren't all of us

Young and able to split, hammer, haul, plant, saw, push,
                              carry, lift, and
At the end of the physical day simply and sublimely sit?

We breathed the dank clean air, the thin sharp smells of
                              pine woods and dead
Leaves and melting snow, and we started to whoop and jig
                              for the vision of it,
The earth strength that we had lived too long without.

What brought me to the woods was grief. My mother died of cancer when I was twenty-one. She was forty-eight. Hers was a protracted, harrowing death with remissions, tatters of hope, experimental treatments, and deep stretches of agony alleviated by morphine oblivion. For six years she was in and out of hospitals. I walked the long linoleum corridors and talked with the doctors, interns, and nurses about dosages and the weather, about radiation and baseball, about surgery and traffic jams. For every dire perplexity a mundane tangent beckoned.

I sat by her bedside reading aloud to her from her favorite distraction—Victorian novels. She was wild about Anthony Trollope. The vicars and lords and widows whose cordial yet machinating lives Trollope recounted seemed reasonably settled, yet being people they managed to muck things up. Both the settled aspect, the golden dust of autumnal England, the material weight of furniture and dresses and jewels, and the making a mess of things pleased my mother. She had lived, but she wanted to live more. She had wanted to visit Europe and view cathedrals and parsonages. She had wanted to breathe the ripe air of history. Now there were a hospital bed and duration and books.

I lived with death on a daily basis, a companion of sorts, mute but tireless. When I shaved in the morning or stopped at a drive-in to get a hamburger or walked from one class at the university to another, I felt death's presence. In that sense, part of me was dying with her as I watched her valiantly struggle with her disease's mindless depredations. What did those dispiriting cancer cells know? How many nights had I sat by her bedside when she was asleep, too weary and sad to pick myself up, and listened to the noises of the hospital, the squeak of shoes and the rolling creak of gurneys, as if they might bring me an answer?

What brought me to the woods was the prospect of living with nothing between me and the earth—none of the electronic gibber-jabber. I craved directness and quiet. What brought me to the woods was an impulse to get lost, to almost literally be off the map. America was a vast country. A fair amount of it still looked as though not many people lived there. I liked the prospect of thinking about land not in terms of building lots but as acres. What brought me to the woods was generational. My wife and I were part of the Back-to-the-Land Movement of the sixties and seventies, the little tide of people who wanted to return to a countryside they had never experienced. What brought me to the woods was romanticism. I wanted to feel elemental sublimity, the full force of the stars and rain and wind. What brought me to the woods was pragmatism. I wanted to learn how to take care of myself. What brought me to the woods was my being an urban Jew who was ready to leave behind the vestiges of assimilated religion and culture that had been bequeathed to me. I wasn't ashamed of it. I craved, however, something different from the largely asphalt landscape I grew up in. What brought me to the woods was the longing to be with words in an undistracted place. "Woods" and "words" were almost identical.

When we look for one thread of motive, we are, in all likelihood, deceiving ourselves.

Our family lived for over twenty-three years on forty-eight wooded acres that we purchased from an old Mainer who had bought up land in the thirties like postage stamps and occasionally sold a parcel when he needed to raise some cash. We lived off the grid—no conventional power, no electric lines, no light switches, no faucets or spigots, no toaster or hair dryer, no flush toilet, no furnace, no hot water heater, and no monthly bill from Central Maine Power. Often when we told people how we lived, they asked us forthrightly how we could live that way. What was with us? Frequently they assumed that we were ideologues, that we were living without electricity as a statement about the excesses of modern times, that our lives were an accusation against everyone else. Maybe we were latter day Luddites or devotees of Rousseau or the Shakers. We must be of the company of the sanctimonious, those who live to judge others.

I never blamed scoffers for making such assumptions. Anything out of the ordinary tends to be taken personally. It wasn't that we set out to live off the grid, nor did we feel we had to live on the grid. We were loose. We situated our house a few hundred feet beyond what the power company considered a reasonable distance to put in their poles. Beyond that distance, a customer had to sign a contract and pay a hefty sum up front. Lacking that money, we went powerless. We could have placed the house closer to the poles—there was plenty of road frontage—but that logical consideration never entered our heads. Other concerns—aesthetic, intuitive, and earthy—guided where we built our house. We chose a rise where, once upon a time, a farmhouse had sat. Despite the rapidity with which a dooryard reverted to woods, there was a remnant of a south-facing clearing. We had rented our share of dark apartments and wanted all the sunlight we could get. People had lived for eons without electric lights and water pressure. Shakespeare and Cleopatra had gotten by. Though we had never done it, as blithe and hardworking spirits we felt that we could, too.

At first we said, "Next year, we'll get power. This is just temporary." Years went by, however, and we got used to going to the outhouse, hauling buckets of water, heating with wood, bathing in a metal tub, lighting kerosene lamps. A small gas stove ran off propane tanks; we cooked on it when the wood-fired cook stove wasn't in use. We never set out to be purists. The simplicity of our lives, how physical action A produced result B, pleased us more than it tired us. Nor did we expect anyone to be particularly enthused about how we lived. Most Americans believe in progress of some type; going backward seems perverse. Though we had our material enthusiasms—hand tools, cast-iron cookware, blue jeans, and ceramic vases, among other things—the way we lived took some air out of the sails of modern, technological desire. An amused friend called us "cheerleaders for the days of yore."

I tended to take heart from what Hazel in Flannery O'Connor's *Wise Blood* said. His landlady was upset about the mortifications that Hazel practiced. It was medieval, something no one did anymore: "It's like one of them gory stories, it's something people have quit doing—like boiling in oil or being a saint or walling up cats." To this Hazel responded, "They ain't quit doing it as long as I'm doing it." All it takes is one naïve, committed, or stubborn person to undo any behavioral law. Although not stubborn, we definitely were naïve and committed.

❧

We built our shingled Cape at the end of a dirt road in a rural community in central Maine. Beyond our house were hundreds of acres of trees dotted here and there with long-abandoned farmsteads. In the nineteenth century and well into the twentieth, virtually all the land around us, including our own, had been field. Our town had been a patchwork of small farms—cows and crops. Now it was mixed woods, the camaraderie of pines and poplars.

It was a rare day when we didn't go for a walk in the woods or on an abandoned road. One road directly in back of our house was used as a snowmobile and ATV trail and was relatively clear. Walking along that road, we could see low stone walls that stretched in every direction and showed where the fields once had been. The ground within the walls was relatively flat. There were no sloughs or holes where tree stumps had been. Someone had leveled and plowed it. We could imagine the cattle and sheep and horses, the barns and troughs and cribs, the attentive rituals that animal care entails. We could imagine the land in different seasons. Once there had been a whole world of horse-drawn sleighs. It had happened right where we stood—before Ford's Model A ever came down the road.

The stone walls had been carefully built. Despite many decades of neglect and frost heaves, most walls sat there staunchly. A round stone or two might have tumbled here and there, but that was the exception rather than the rule. Similarly, the walls of the abandoned cellar holes into which we peered were largely intact. We marveled at the weight and size of the cut granite blocks and the teams of oxen that must have hauled them. We wondered how the builders had maneuvered the blocks into place without the huge cranes that today we take for granted. An old-timer told us we would be surprised what a couple of pulleys could do.

So much precision and responsibility, and all abandoned. How bittersweet it was. We had moved to a place that seemed to be forgotten, a place people inevitably left. The nation at large beckoned, and during the twentieth century, as the economics of small farms became impossible, people gave up on this place. By the time we arrived, the backcountry farmhouses had caved in along with the barns, the sheds, the chicken coops. Some days when we looked at the heaps of gray, weather-beaten lumber and the scattering of busted crockery and rusted pots, it seemed as though people had left in the middle of the night before an advancing army. They hadn't, however. This was America. They left for a better life.

It was unsettling to become so aware of what had been lost. We fingered the patent medicine bottles, hinges, stove lids, hasps, and nails as if we were archeologists of the soul. Who had these people been? Their descendents were living in Florida and California and Texas and perhaps had stories in their families of grandparents who once had lived in Maine. Or perhaps shame and silent grief had accompanied the generation as it left the land. Yankees were reticent to begin with. They didn't confess or blubber. "Times got tough," or "the war came along" would be enough of an explanation. It was hard to know. America was so huge on possibility and so scant on the quiet suffering of history. Who wanted the blues of loss? Americans were boosters not lamenters. Newcomers to ruin, we picked up an intact bottle, took it to our house, cleaned out the dirt, and set it on a windowsill as a totem, keepsake, and reminder.

Not much seemed to happen in the woods. In autumn, the leaves and needles came down. They did this variously as many verbs beginning with the letter *f* attested—fall, flutter, fly, feint, float, frolic, flit, flail. For a few weeks in October, transience created a moment-by-moment spectacle. In pointillist May, the trees would begin to fledge pale, almost translucent greens that slowly and steadily revealed themselves. To the casual, accustomed eye that remarked upon large-scale events, nothing much was happening.

That meant that we lived in the woods for over two decades and never saw a black bear. Occasionally we noticed a set of unmistakable tracks that revealed a slow or fast lope. Every summer we saw blackberry and raspberry canes bent over every which way. Bears had been pillaging patches that had grown up where logging had occurred. We saw fresh scats; once in a long while we noticed pines whose bark had been peeled off to get at the sap; but we never saw a bear. This lack of a sighting as we went our irregular rounds pleased me more than it disappointed. The woods were mysterious and vast. The creatures that lived there went about their business. Like people, they came and went, prospered and waned. If we had shown up at the beginning of the twentieth century, we would have encountered very few wild creatures because, out of need, commerce, sport, and sheer wantonness, humans had shot or trapped most of them. As it was, their lives had their own orbits. Avoiding us, as we galumphed along talking about politics or a book we had read and smelling like the oily humans we were, was part of it. The bears were succeeding.

The life occurring around us was small-scale but intense; I came to love the feeling that the woods were alive with an energy I couldn't hear or see. Even when I could hear that energy, as when the cicadas buzzed in high summer, I still couldn't see it. For those hot, drowsy weeks the air sizzled with sound. Mostly it was quiet in the woods, yet the work of digesting matter was ongoing. If I took note of some fir or pine that had blown down in a big wind and came back from summer to summer to observe it, I could trace its progress back to the soil. Even before the bark began to loosen, dry up, and flake off, platoons of beetles showed up. I admired the ingenious tunnels, cavities, and holes they made. Sometimes I peeled off a strip of bark and found "frass," little powdery deposits of digested wood. Time seemed palpable to me. It was what was chewed up. If on a summer's day you sat by a downed trunk that had been out in the weather for a few years, you could hear borers munching away. "Determined as a beetle" seemed a good simile to me.

When we saw certain animals, a moose or otter or bobcat, it was a special event—like a coronation. We were pleased and excited, but most days we saw nothing out of the ordinary. The hemlock branches swayed in the wind—green filigree. Boulders sat still for the millennia that dwarfed our days. Ants ran along the earth full of what seemed like purpose. Robins patrolled our patch of mowed lawn. Paper wasps built nests and fed on the pollen of goldenrod. The ordinary was, of course, hardly ordinary. Who could imagine in his or her head even a fraction of what any acre of any woods or field held? In a wet September we would walk in back of our house and gawk at the mushrooms. Where had they all come from?

※

Like most people who grew up in the United States after World War II, I thought of indoor light as a matter of flicking a switch. Electricity was current and currency. I had never seriously thought of life without it. Now and then the villages in Africa or Asia I saw in photos in *National Geographic* reminded me that people were living without outlets and poles, but such worlds seemed inherently exotic and almost unearthly. There were no cars in those pictures, fast-food containers, record albums, or refrigerators. Often someone with deep-set, expressive eyes was staring into the photographer's expensive lens. So much feeling simmered in such a face that the practicalities of daily life—getting water, bathing, cooking food, being able to see when it got dark—vanished. Or what informed that face was the experience of deeper practicalities, ones I couldn't, as I sat in a dentist's fluorescent waiting room, fathom.

I remember the evening of the first day in which we moved into our house in the woods. It started to get dark, and I thought—it is getting dark. That seems simple-minded, but what I felt was vividly complex. Night's coming was so profound, so transfixing, so soft yet indelible that I was startled and lulled in the same awed moment. I remember very clearly feeling how, second by tiny second, it was getting darker, how the dark was creeping in, how it was inexorable and delicate, how night "fell"—a great, slow curtain—how darkness "grew"—something organic yet rooted in the ineffable. Poets had written endlessly about the melancholy and charm of

9

dusk; it was the time of haunting regret—another day never to be seen again. I could feel that mood as I moved about the house and watched the waning light. It was fluid, like ink in water, and calmly eerie. There was no switch to hit to banish the dark, to create a clear divide, to join the bright ranks of the electrified world.

We lit kerosene lamps. One hung from a beam in the kitchen area, several were mounted on walls, and a few sat on tables. The ones on the walls were small, glass ones that were still commonly sold in Maine hardware stores. The lamp's base sat in a metal holder that fit into a bracket. The one on our dining table was ceramic with pink flowers and light green leaves painted all around. The large one on our kitchen counter had a pedestal; it was glass, ornate, and semi-antique. When the inside of the house seemed too dark to move around in, we lit the lamps. It was an intuitive moment because, over time, we got very used to darkness. The lamps lit only relatively small areas, so the house, which was one big room downstairs and a sleeping loft upstairs, held plenty of shadowy places. We moved in and out of the bright spaces that the little lights created; we felt darkness as an eminence, a deep totality, an extinction of the ever-glad sun. When we looked out the window, there was unrelieved night. The moon and stars were cold, clear, unearthly light.

The attractiveness of the kerosene lamps—even the glass ones were stamped on their sides with some scene in relief of sentimentalized rural life (a fancy, horse-drawn carriage, for instance) or swirls of foliage—belied their drawbacks. Coal oil has a strong, unlovely smell; we usually had a window partially open to air the house out. The wicks had to be trimmed regularly, the chimneys had to be cleaned when they got sooty, and, of course, the lamps had to be replenished. That meant filling a five-gallon can at the local store and lugging it back to the small storage shed behind the house. That meant going out in all weather to fill the lamps. That meant an occasional spill and the crude, seemingly imperishable odor of kerosene on my hands or gloves. Light did not materialize of itself. Our efforts each day made it happen. A match had to be struck. Our heedlessness had a limit.

We were aware that kerosene was the outcome of an industrial process. Our life in the woods was not in the service of a noble myth. Kerosene was available; we used it accordingly. A few guests over the years found the stench appalling and the light feeble. As much as they wanted to be charmed, they weren't. I loved lying in bed and reading by the light of a small kerosene lamp. I was reading in the presence of an actual flame. I could feel that flame every second as it raggedly danced. Time was steady, but in the flame's movements it varied. That feeling was as precious as the poems I read almost every night.

The lamps were fussy, for the wicks had to be adjusted to throw the most light without blackening the chimney. I took this attentiveness as one of the gifts that simple living provided. The lamps and the poems were really the same. They were a sweet labor. They formed shapes that were predictable yet unique. They were alive. When I looked at the house from the outside as I was coming back from the woodshed or outhouse, there was a soft glow inside it. Many a time that glow stopped me in my tracks, it was so beautiful. All around was forested darkness, but the house shone gently.

It was a romantic glow. The romantic impulse is often disparaged; we fear the treachery of feeling. It's safer to dwell in the domains of irony. We cut short our losses because we cut short our longings. We parade our adjustment and disillusion as triumphs. We mock ourselves to forestall the world's mockery. The romantic impulse believes that there is an extraordinary amount of feeling available each moment. The trembling light is quietly breathtaking. It causes soot and stench; it came from the hard work of mining, processing, and trucking and is not particularly effective in lighting a large space. All true, but the feeling remains. Touch the glass chimney—it is hot with the heat that signals light. A poem, as it embodies emotion that is both modulated and fervent, possesses human heat and light. It speaks to an ache deep within us. If we take poetry down some pegs by insisting on its limitations, we diminish its force. We wind up the poorer for our comfort.

In the kitchen area beside the porcelain sink that a friend had scavenged stood a small, iron, pitcher pump. This pump pulled water up, stroke by stroke, from the dug well in our front yard. A dug well is just what it says—a well that has been dug in the ground. Before backhoes came along, they were dug with a pick and shovel and lined with stones. When we first moved into our house, we used the well that had been the water source for the farmhouse that had stood close by. Looking down it was not so much vertiginous—the well wasn't very deep—as mysterious. Moss lined the stones; small frogs frolicked on the sides. We saw snakes. When we thought about what little creatures might be decomposing at the bottom of the well, we decided to pump it out and cover it with a cement cap.

Eventually we decided to dig another well, as the old well tended to go dry in a rainless summer. We were hoping to find a stronger vein of sweet water. Understandably, people in the country are very attuned to water. You can't have a house without it; a spring is especially prized. We, who had come to the country to experience country ways, had a dowser come to witch for water. He brought a wishbone-shaped length of alder and walked very slowly through the clearing in which our house stood, the stick held out and slightly upward from his waist. A lanky old Scotsman, he was part hydrologist ("Water is everywhere underground") and part mystic ("The water in the earth calls to the water in the wood"). The stick dipped perceptibly when he was around ten feet from where the old well was. We had a contractor dig there, but the source was not much better. It was a chance we took; we chalked it up as another rural experience. Watching the stick bend downwards had been strange and thrilling—not like anything we had ever witnessed. The paranormal didn't entice us, but we didn't believe the human mind was an accurate measurer of the universe either. The dowser didn't charge us money for his services. He was doing "the work God wants me to do on this green earth."

It didn't take much water for our household to get by. We had an outhouse, so there was no flushing. We washed our hair over the sink by pouring water from a pot we dipped into a bucket. When we showered, we used a solar black bag that could wash you quite thoroughly with a few quarts of water. Or, if we were feeling expansive, we filled an oval metal tub. To sit in the tub when we placed it in front of the open oven door of the wood-fired cook stove and let the warmth pour out was downright sensual. Daily we heated our wash water on that cook stove or the little gas stove. We had clear, clean, delicious water to drink and cook with. Our clothes got done each week at the Laundromat. We practiced an economy that was not a hardship.

Despite such modest use, one droughty fall we ran out. I bought a couple of ten-gallon containers and filled them up at our neighbors' house a half mile down the road. Their outside faucet froze up in November, but a fellow teacher in the town where I worked let me use his kitchen tap. Joe had grown up the old-fashioned way—outhouse and no running water—and thought we were hopeless fools to embrace such inconvenience. I would place the hard plastic containers in his kitchen sink and listen to stories about growing up in Maine in the thirties. According to Joe, the Depression had been a step up for his town in northern Maine because government people came along and handed out free fishing poles. And here we were—trying to live as though we were in the Depression all over again. Joe taught very eclectic English classes that included as required reading Thomas Pynchon and Nelson Algren. His taste ran to "gritty absurdity," as he put it; my own life demonstrated that there was no accounting for how human beings acted.

After filling up, I would trudge out the door, both hands on the container's handle, and try not to slip, throw my back out, or have the sheer momentum of the weight propel me into the street in front of Joe's house. I'd hoist the water into the back of the Subaru wagon and thank Joe. "Come anytime," he'd say, then shake his large, crew-cut head at the oddness of it all. "I knew if I lived long enough the wheel would come around." He'd shake his head again.

I liked driving home and hearing the water slosh around. It sounded cozy. I liked knowing that now our family had enough water to get by for a number of days. Then I'd be back in Joe's kitchen hearing about the time his father got a job on the Canadian

Pacific Railroad or how the problem with public education was that we'd given up on Latin.

The next fall was also dry. Joe was going through a bad divorce, not around much, and not in a good mood when he was around. We decided to drill a well. Usually when wells are drilled, they are hooked up to electric pumps. Since we had no electricity, we installed a piston pump that pushed the water up. A standard push-down-on-a-long-arm sort of pump, it was called "Columbiana" and was named for an Ohio town where the pump was made. You see them sometimes at campsites. It usually took three or four lusty downward pumps, and water started gushing—first a little surge and then a real bonanza. We put a bucket underneath and hauled water bucket by bucket. It tasted of granite and wasn't as sweet as the dug well, but it served our purposes. It went down the better part of two hundred feet and never showed signs of going dry. Then again, we never used that much.

Summer was when we used the most, for we watered our large vegetable garden and several flower gardens bucket by bucket. I spent countless hours lugging water. I could have rigged something up to the pump that would use a hose, but I had no mechanical imagination. Plus, the fact was that I liked to lug water. It was slow and peaceful; I liked gently watering plants from a watering can. It was another meditative task, a chance to get lost in simplicity. In the early evening I'd be out there pumping away. I'd read that water carriers were integral parts of the community in the Pale of Settlement my Russian grandmother came from. I figured that I was a latter-day descendant: the spirit of some Shmuel or Moishe was alive in me.

Since manual labor is rarely, if ever, remunerated properly, the water carrier was probably not an esteemed benefactor to the local synagogue. That lowly person may have been a dreamer or a ne'er-do-well or someone who was saving his pennies to come to America and become something more than a beast of burden in a muddy, fly-blown village. Regardless of such imaginings, the pump spoke to me. "Here," the pump said, "is water. It comes from the earth and the sky. Consider the mystery that you take for granted." Every time I moved the pump arm up and down, up and down, I encountered that feeling. At first nothing seemed to be happening in the pump—some whooshes of air, some clanging metal—and then there it was from deep in the earth—water. I found myself staring down at the slowly filling bucket or putting my hand out to feel that first, cold splash. In the hot summer we squatted naked beneath the pump and let the water numb us. In the winter we struggled with ice, with snow that buried the pump, and with below-zero temperatures that would freeze it solid. Yet it would thaw eventually. Water would return. Bucket by bucket, I would carry it.

The poet Lionel Johnson is supposed to have said to William Butler Yeats that he, Johnson, needed to spend ten years in the wilderness whereas Yeats needed to spend ten years in a library. Yeats, of course, as a young Romantic poet, favored the wilderness of the heart and the unrequited wilderness of the Celtic past. Though well read, Yeats feared the dustiness of libraries, the specter of the don who buried poetry beneath the sedulous weight of scholarship. Johnson, who was a polished poet, realized that he could have used some time outside his sadly comfortable world of drink.

When I read of this exchange in Richard Ellmann's biography of Yeats, I felt a twinge of recognition. I was working in a library in an area that certainly would have qualified as wilderness beside the groomed fields and manor houses of Ireland. North of town the vast woods of Maine began in earnest. Many parcels of that area were designated not by names but by numbers and letters like T3 R11. They constituted "unorganized territory." The pulp trucks that came barreling down the state highways to the paper mills testified to how many more trees there were than people.

Yet, as a librarian, I spent each day with books—handing them out, locating them, reading about them, looking them over, and talking about them. For my students I represented the world of books. They had plenty of questions; I had plenty of somewhat idiosyncratic answers. When I pointed at the long wall of novels in the library, I told them that these were all sad stories—a wall of sad stories about human miscomprehension. Where were the happy books? Not on the wall of Dostoevsky and Kate Chopin and Balzac and Stephen Crane; not in the genre that stressed the wages our socialized lives extracted. The books on the wall could be humorous, but they were not happy. I told my students that they would have to make their peace with unhappiness. That was part of being an adult—not renouncing happiness but making one's peace with unhappiness. My students were patient with me—that was, after all, a large part of being a student, being patient with adults. "I just wanted a recommendation, Mr. Wormser, not a lecture about life," was what I saw in more than one student's eyes. That was fair enough. I always complimented them on their choices. Any choice could change any life.

Each day I considered books of all sorts—novels that once had been acclaimed but now were sliding into oblivion (Paul Gallico, Norman Douglas, Irving Stone), reference books that sat waiting sedately for one idle or earnest question, encyclopedias that inoffensively summarized revolutions and assassinations, nonfiction books about vandalism and archery and tropical fish and Jane Addams and growing up black in South Africa and on and endlessly on. Routinely, I read hundreds upon hundreds of book reviews. Out of that articulate ocean I chose a few books. The library was small enough (around twelve thousand volumes) to give a manageable sense of the whole span of the human endeavor. In my amateur, groping way I became familiar with everything.

The great Borges had been a librarian. It was easy to see why. Although librarians in America were as keen on whiz-bang technology as anyone was, there remained a certain literal dustiness to the vocation, a fascination with the mind's alleyways, boulevards, and dead ends. Even a dull book was the product of some species of imagination. And the relations among the books, the strange neighbors that libraries created, the fraught decisions that my students made each day in choosing books and that I made in selecting them gave off a small, metaphysical quiver. The gruff dispensation of the alphabet put Jane Austen, Chinua Achebe, Sherwood Anderson, and Kingsley Amis within hailing distance of one another. If the categorizing that typified a library came to seem logical, that was one more trick of the human mind. Within such order lurked senselessness, profundity, and whimsy, as Borges well knew. A library was a metaphor for the human endeavor come to life, a finite collection that opened infinite vistas. Who could follow the silent paths of minds as they devoured sentence after sentence? The words disappeared into the reader yet never left the printed page. As I purchased, catalogued, weeded, and recommended, I created something very quietly alive.

At home I read more. There was a total of two other houses on the mile or so of our road; our social life could have been described as modest. For a decade we did not even have a telephone. Wherever the cultural center of things may have been, we were far away from it. While lying in bed at night and reading Henry James, I heard coyotes howling. If the U.S.A. is the land of collisions, of one dissimilarity encountering another and trying to get along, then my situation seemed, despite its remoteness, archetypal. The glorified cabin in the woods (as our son somewhat acerbically and somewhat lovingly came to call it), the weird, almost unreal yips of animal excitement, and the words of the Master: what did they have to do with one another? James had left his homeland and, decorous though he was, didn't skimp on reasons to prefer ancient, settled Europe to the anxious, inventive bustle of the States. The internal wilderness of human beings was sufficient subject matter. The taming of the external wilderness was bound to be rude and laborious, the stuff of braggadocio. I blew out the kerosene lamp—a small, quick, taut exhalation—and turned toward my sleeping wife. I thought of the ceaseless, self-conscious artistry of James's words, of his genius for querying the smooth wheels of duplicity: the more that was said, the more went unsaid. As I pulled the flannel sheets over me, I heard howls that belied words.

We resolved to build our house ourselves. Though my wife had studied architecture for a time and was a capable designer, the world of practical carpentry was a mystery to us. We knew what a two-by-four was and what a hammer was, but we didn't own a Skil saw, much less a table saw. Perhaps we would do the whole thing with a handsaw and an ax. What did we know? We had read a do-it-yourself book or two that showed how houses were built. We would follow the instructions just as we did when we encountered a new recipe. As college graduates we could learn whatever we had to learn.

It's hard for me to fathom how simple-minded yet determined we were. I look back at us at the beginning of our sojourn in the woods as somewhat holy fools—serendipity will provide. It did. Illumination, to say nothing of practical help, appeared in the form of a Maine carpenter and jack-of-most-trades named Caleb. Word must have gotten out in the neighborhood that some hippies were building a house or camp or cabin or something utterly unspeakable in the woods. Caleb was curious enough to brave the morass of our road. He got out of his battered, mid-1950s pickup and sauntered up to our site, a man in his early sixties with a limp, a potbelly, a ruddy complexion, and very steady blue eyes. We (which meant myself, Janet, and her younger brother Dave) were pondering the mysteries of concrete—not actually pouring any, but pondering it. We had the old dug well from which to draw water. We had a wheelbarrow to mix the stuff, and we had a lot of empty tubes to fill on which the house would reside. Due to heavy rains, the holes in which those tubes sat were mostly full of water. Small frogs were hopping about everywhere with what seemed like great abandon.

Caleb's Maine accent had a musical twang. His voice moved slightly up and down as he spoke his introductions, though his tone was steadily bemused. We chatted about the weather (we all agreed it had been rainy) and how it seemed as though more and more young people were moving to Maine. Then, very politely, Caleb looked the scene over and asked us in a mild, wry voice if we had ever built a house before. "Well, not really," we replied. We didn't even bother with some qualifying "but." "How," he asked after a brief, respectful pause in which he tugged at the visor of his green cap, "would you like me to build this for you? Take a couple of weeks. A jiffy." He halted. "You can help." My wife and I deliberated for a few seconds before nodding wholeheartedly. Caleb smiled a false-toothed smile. "We'll get her up before you know it. You just see." We talked over a few details about mixing concrete and what we had for lumber. Caleb shook our hands; he was missing the tips of two fingers on his right hand. Then he headed back to his truck. We never talked money.

The next day we started very early—around six. Caleb favored the cool hours of the morning. He'd get up in the dark of four or five a.m., eat a bowl of oatmeal, then head off to work. He was still very strong; when he worked it was with a kind of reckless determination. I'd never until that day seen anyone work the way Caleb worked. He kept moving constantly while directing Dave and me (we were manning the wheelbarrows) and two of his relatives (a grandson and grandson-in-law) who knew how to carpenter. He didn't pause. He didn't look around. I don't even recall him excusing himself to take a leak behind a tree. I was surprised he didn't finish the whole job in a day. As it was, we poured all the concrete and started cutting the sills that day. If he hadn't been so good-natured, I would have thought he was possessed. Dave and I collapsed with fatigue as soon as he left.

The Maine that we wanted to be close to was personified in Caleb. He had finished school after seventh grade ("had enough of sittin' at a desk") and had gone to work in the woods. He had worked in lumber camps and carpentered his whole life. Though various construction companies had employed him, he preferred being his own boss. He loved to build rough structures—barns, chicken houses, outbuildings. Finish carpentry held no allure for him; his favorite phrase was "close enough—spike it." An eighth of an inch didn't keep him awake at night. Though he used a spirit level, he didn't let it deter him.

Caleb lived down the road from us and, with his devout wife, had raised six daughters. He never went to church ("for women") but was a clean-living man. "I seen too much of what liquor does to people." Caleb believed in the gospel of work. Until he knocked off around three o'clock, his energy never flagged. Then he went home, took a brief nap, accepted visits from his enormous clan, ate dinner, and read a tattered Western by the likes of Zane Gray before turning in around eight. He was at it again the next morning at six.

Like a number of old-timers we were to meet, Caleb had little use for authority. That's where, despite our very different backgrounds and despite our ages, we clicked. We never talked politics for a second. There wasn't much need to. Caleb had little use for anyone in a suit and tie. "What kind of work can a man do in a suit and tie?" Caleb snorted. He had never voted. He wasn't proud of it, nor was he ashamed. To get excited about promises from people you'd never met was wishful at best, childish at worst. A speech was puffery; anyone could tell people what they wanted to hear. Anyone could wave a placard and cheer. To an independent Yankee cuss like Caleb, the very notion of cheering seemed ludicrous. He was that bracing blend we were to come across in rural Maine of the upright and the anarchistic. His moral code was utter honesty and frank contempt for anyone who didn't live up to that code. He wasn't cut out for latter-day, corporate America, and he knew it. That was fine with him. As long as he could limp along (his hip was going) and work, he was happy.

What Caleb liked to do during lunch or while we were waiting for the lumber truck to show up was tell stories. He had been all over New England as a young man. If he didn't like a situation, he left that situation. Once when he was walking down the main street of a town in northern Maine, he realized he only had a quarter to his name. Caleb promptly threw it away because he'd earn that and more. He had eaten every food known to man. "Ever eat woodchuck, Red?" he asked me one day. "Worst knot in my stomach I ever had." A great bestower of nicknames, Caleb had deemed me "Red" for my hair and my brother-in-law "Lightning" for his sometimes dilatory work habits. Caleb had never gone West, but he was a part of that American restlessness that always had to be doing something. The only stillness he recognized was fatigue. He loved exertion, but he also loved the thinking that went before the exertion. He was ever considering what had to be done next. For all his bluff ways, he was thoughtful.

Our modest, Cape-style house was done in a month, and not

long afterward we moved in with our two-year-old daughter. Featuring cedar shakes from a local mill, six-over-six windows, and a back porch with hemlock posts I had cut in the forest, it was a testament to the beauty of wood. Caleb came by regularly to check on us. There was no telling what such naïfs might do. He would wink at us when he inquired how we were getting along. We had no idea what we were up against. He did but never let on. From the outset he understood us; our romanticism appealed to his. Despite his air of practicality, he loved the freedom of following his own nose. That was how he'd shown up in the first place. It was as if he'd been waiting.

⁂

When I was an undergraduate, I read Robert Frost's "The Need of Being Versed in Country Things." The poem moved me, yet I wondered about so many things. I wondered about the notion of "need" in the title. Why did anyone need this? And what did it mean to be "versed" in something? Used to? In the know? And what was a phoebe? I asked the teaching assistant if he knew what a phoebe was. He looked quizzically at me. He was witty and loved to take our first perceptions and turn them upside down. I liked paradox and enjoyed his showmanship; literature was meat for his intellect. He didn't, however, know what a phoebe was. "Some bird," he mumbled. "I sort of guessed that," I replied. He smiled faintly and went on about Frost and the neo-pastoral.

I sat there wondering about the bird. I knew robins and crows and blue jays. That was about it. My hometown bird, the Baltimore oriole, was an uncommon sight thanks to DDT and the death of the elms they loved to nest in. As to what a phoebe was, it fell in the same category as Coleridge's albatross. Seen an albatross lately? Seen a phoebe lately? I thought of Holden Caulfield's young sister. Wasn't she named Phoebe? I knew that nothing in Salinger was left to chance. There was the mythic echo, too. I looked up and heard the word "Virgilian" come out of my instructor's mouth.

On the north side of our house in the woods there was a ledge beneath the roof overhang that Caleb never bothered to box in. Like us, our home was a work in progress. Our second spring in the house I noticed some intense nest building going on—two birds of rather unremarkable color, sort of gray over green. I looked in my bird guide. Phoebes. No question about it, these were phoebes fluttering around and carrying in their bills grass and little tufts of moss and bits of dirt. When they sat on a branch of a nearby maple, they wagged their tail feathers—up and down, then a pause, then up and down again. It was endearing in the manner of a charming anxiety, an avian tic.

Phoebes, we learned, like to nest on human habitations. As birds go, they are very tame; our watching them at their work gave them little concern. They felt free to go about their business, which was breeding and raising their young and catching insects and flying away and returning again next year—for they did come back, year after year. We made a point of removing nests, because they sometimes would start to build upon an old nest and leave themselves no room to fly in beneath the overhang. We looked forward to their coming each spring.

Birds are variously conjugal. The phoebes seemed to us to be exemplars of a good marriage. They were always together, and we imagined them as parents—trying to find the right materials to construct a nest, fussing endlessly, feeding the ever-hungry chicks, keeping an eye out as the fledglings grew restive to leave the nest, planning for next year. We were indulging in anthropomorphism, but the phoebes invited it. The bird world and the human world didn't seem that different. Out of all the structures they could have chosen, they chose ours. We were proud.

What was it to be versed? I didn't know but wanted to learn. However opaquely, I sensed that Frost's concerns were similar to mine, that writing poetry and living in the country were the same enterprise. Both were about situating one's self—be it in the lines of poems or on the earth among the trees and birds. Being versed had to do with being situated, with dwelling. The turning that is at the root of the Latin word *versus* was a turning into a situation, an entering of a certain kind of being. Frost, of course, went in fear of even common abstractions like "being." He trusted that the actualities—deer, streams, apples, stars, snow—were verity enough; then he spent a lifetime testing that trust. His greatest poems offered the hardest tests. He sought to be fair and to refuse false consolation; he managed to be relentless and wry at the same time. Although in his poem people were no longer there, the phoebes did return. Perhaps those people had delighted in the phoebes as we had. It was a reasonable surmise; they were birds that seemed to invite feeling. Though Frost was shrewd, he honored feeling as much as any poet.

Those "country things" of which Frost wrote were a deep learning. To try to paraphrase what they were was bound to end in failure because they were like the Taoist Ten Thousand Things. They were the rudiments of life as lived by all the different creatures—not just humans. They formed an incredible network or web or weave or whatever metaphor one chose. The life spirit goes on as it builds nests; our human attentions are so much chatter heard at a distance. Then, as had happened on the farms that once existed all around us, that chatter disappears. Instinct is in all creatures, but our human feeling is sifted inexorably by our wanting and our knowing. One wouldn't choose to renounce that tangle, but one wouldn't aim to make too much of it either. Frost's hand was remarkably delicate and firm at the same time. To write "Not to believe the phoebes wept" was to touch something almost more than the eager human mind could bear. He allowed for the poignancy, and he allowed for the indifference of vitality. "For them there was nothing really sad." One had to be versed. . . .

※

When my first book of poetry appeared, the Portland paper ran a feature on me with a banner announcing, "Small Town Librarian Hits Poetry Big Time." Beyond the amusement afforded by the bodacious fizz of headline writing, the words raised the curious issue of being a poet in the United States. What was that? Something to emblazon on one's T-shirts? Something to hide? Something to bring out only in the company of fellow travelers? Something accessible? Something academic? Something recondite? All of the above?

I came to poetry through a love of reading poetry. Night after kerosene night I read Frost and Shakespeare and Donne and Dickinson and was very happy doing so. I wrote no papers nor kept a journal, talked occasionally with my wife about a poem or read her some lines, and kept reading. I was entranced. The feeling of how much could happen in such a small space was heady. The ardor of the enterprise, the mix of daring and composure compelled me in a way nothing else quite compelled me. Over and over I could witness these bravura performances. Over and over I felt how a mere word could move me as much as a struck piano key. Words were notes, too, and vibrated accordingly. I would put down a book and stare into space for minutes. "Okay over there?" my wife would ask. "Okay," I would reply. Somehow these people had found ways to communicate the very thrill of being alive (and of facing death) through language. Poetry resided in that thrill.

I could see where an adult might not want that thrill. Habitual and out-of-the-ordinary losses posed questions for which there were no answers. Why seek further in the beautiful badlands of poems? And what could one do with those poems? How did one communicate them to others? For my octogenarian neighbor, Stanton, who had been made to memorize pages of Whittier and Longfellow as a boy and who could still repeat those pages, the answer was simple—one quoted lines from those poems to people whenever the topic of poetry came up or when the moment struck him as poetically appropriate. For Stanton, poetry stopped there. Those poems were talismans—he knew there was such a thing as poetry, and he knew some poems by heart, and that was all that needed to be said about it. What the twentieth century went and did was the twentieth century's problem. That it turned its back on the moralizing, ballad-influenced poem that had once been as common as pennies made it all the worse.

Stanton never would have picked up my headline-garnering book; I can't say I knew many people in Somerset County who would. I didn't take the lack of attention personally. After all, the writing had started for me quite adventitiously. I hadn't gone to any academic setting to pursue an advanced degree. I didn't harbor notions of a career. What happened was disarmingly mundane: my wife took the children for a visit to her parents' house in Massachusetts. After unrelieved years of the blab, thump, whine, shriek, and giggle of two young children, I had a few silent days to myself. That weekend I started writing poems. I had no idea where they were coming from, but there they were. I had worked on a novel and a book about architecture in my twenties; I enjoyed doing the writing, although neither manuscript had been published. Now there were these poems.

The connection I sensed inside me was that the reading elicited the writing. Something in me wanted to craft those things called poems, the way any made thing—a patchwork quilt, a dadoed bookshelf, a cable-stitch sweater, a honey cake, or an iron poker—might impel a person to make one. I wanted to butt lines up against one another and see how they fit. I wanted to see how the shape determined the line and vice-versa, and how rhythm and sound created what seemed like infinite texture and density within a stanza. I wanted to feel the weight of such a slight thing, for I knew it had a weight and that the weight varied from one stanza to another. I wanted to order the sounds that the syllables and accents made into patterns that pleased me. I wanted the mixed precision of such an endeavor—exact and inexact, steadfast and dreamlike, all at the same time. I wanted to practice balance and imbalance, trace symmetry and asymmetry, toy with words and honor them. Such making offered an expressiveness that went far beyond the perquisites of the blurting, declarative self. The lines could be tuned to a pitch that barely could be heard, yet what Keats termed "a finer tone" reverberated within us.

As to who might consume it, I had no idea. Once poetry left the harbor of a more or less homogeneous rural society, such as Stanton recalled, it found itself on the seas of more contentions and viewpoints than it ever could count. The bewilderment often voiced about poetry seems to stem from nostalgia. Wasn't this poetry stuff all much simpler, once upon a time? One quoted a love poem to one's sweetheart; one basked in the simple, pale glow of sentimentality; one was stirred by patriotism and excited by exploits. What had happened? A brief look at modern times would answer that question many times over, but disillusion rarely has seemed the stuff of inspiration. In fact, the thrill of being alive on earth will never go away, and poetry is steeped in that ardent biology. That thrill— and it is crucial to what makes poetry compelling—is bound to come up against the worlds humankind has created. However intense it may be, a love affair—to cite a standard occasion for writing verse—is not shielded from historical circumstances. Far from it, as *Romeo and Juliet* attests. If poetry wants to flee from such knowledge and celebrate an impossible purity, the impulse is understandable. The words in a poem, after all, are on furlough from daily life. An attention is being paid to them that is uncommon and almost insupportable. Though I had no idea where the stanzas were coming from, they excited me. Though I had no room of my own or even a desk of my own, I did have a pen and a legal pad. To be a part of such a long-standing and deeply human enterprise felt good.

❧

Our house was quite literally in the woods. I cut down poplars, a few spavined apple trees, some white pines, and a number of tall, thin, red maples to create an adequate opening to situate the house and let the sun in over the tree tops. The apple trees must have been the remnant of a little orchard that had been planted near where the farmhouse once stood. The others had grown up randomly as the site of what once was a farm became woods. We used a compass to orient the house to the south. This was not a development lot that had to have its house squarely facing the street. The sun that came up over the trees could be seen from our bedroom window. We could follow it across the front of the house throughout the day. On a frigid but sunny winter day, the south windows suffused a gentle warmth.

In front of and in back of the house stood a number of very straight pines that were fifty to sixty years old. We revered them, though we knew any city person strolling in a park—a domain where aesthetics trumped board feet—would see larger and older trees. In rural Maine lumbering is always an issue; one sees very few, really old trees in the endless woods because those woods are being cut time and time again. The works of man, the industry that drives each economic day, are what the Maine woods call to mind. What man leaves behind is happenstance. The cutters might trust indomitable nature; they might trust cooperative, university-based science; or they might be indifferent.

When I first began to roam the backcountry where we lived, I was routinely appalled when I encountered tracts that had been lumbered recently. Limbs and sections of trunks that were unusable were strewn everywhere. Young trees had been toppled and left eventually to collapse under snow. Splintered trees whose tops had been sheared off when other trees fell on them stood like big, ragged toothpicks. Huge ruts from the skidders that moved the logs were everywhere. Piles of brush sat like so much unwanted debris. It looked like a war had occurred, a war against the trees. Of course, woodcutting isn't an issue of beautification. It's an issue of humankind making a buck off some trees that the rest of humankind needs for paper and lumber. The whole notion of trees as something to regard and venerate would have seemed bizarre to the men with the chainsaws and trucks. The trees were there for people to use. Such is the way of workaday humanity.

We were fortunate. For us, the trees were not part of any crucial, economic equation. When I cut trees for the firewood that kept us warm and that heated our water, I could pick each tree I was going to fell according to how healthy (or unhealthy) the tree was and whether I should thin that one to allow others to grow. I could fell the tree so it would do the least damage to others. I could use virtually the entire tree because I sawed up the limbs for our cook stove. I could arrange the brush on the ground so that it would compact reasonably quickly. You had to take a careful look to notice that a tree had been felled.

Although we heated our house with the trees I cut on our land and although we had no backup heat whatsoever, more than one woodcutter told me that, despite my exertions, I was doing little more in the woods than playing. I could understand. Anything that didn't honor the dollar equation was recreation. Caleb cut trees, sold them for pulp, and used the money to pay for oil heat. He informed me he was "way ahead" by doing this. When I asked him, "Ahead of what?" he only snorted. He had endured a lifetime of starting fires in wood stoves, getting up in the middle of winter nights to put in more wood, then waking in the morning to the cold misery of ashes. I could have it. I was off in my labor-intensive, poetic Oz.

I had to confess that I was quite happy in my Oz of trees. At any time I could walk a few steps and literally be in the woods. In the heat of summer, I had the shade, the coolness, and the ever-changing play of the sifted light. The analogies to a cathedral were not far-fetched. In the heights of the trees there was audible mystery— pewees and tanagers I heard but rarely saw. I marveled at the relentless yearning toward the sun, how the maples made their way amid a canopy of pines. In winter I watched the bare forms gesturing like still dancers. I listened to the spry clatter of branches in a strong wind. They sounded like little bones. In all seasons, the waver and dapple of shadow sighed. When I examined a stump, I saw in the growth rings the shapes of years, some bunched, some even, some protuberant. I was ensorcelled, enchanted, enthralled—all those old, discarded words.

Part of living with the trees lay in considering their ways. Each type of tree was deeply singular. There were the trademark white pines that a friend once likened to huge stalks of celery on account of how their tops waved in a wind. There were the smooth-trunked beeches that held onto their parchment-like leaves throughout the winter and rattled dryly. There were the poplars (or "popple" in the local designation) that were "trash" trees, their loosely fibrous wood considered not good for much of anything. Their diminutive leaves were attuned to every breeze and shimmered with audible movement. In a stiff wind they seemed almost frenetic. There were the deeply furrowed sugar maples along the road to our house that had been tapped to make maple syrup and now were dying as their huge limbs rotted and fell. There were white birches, with their peeling, papery strips of bark, yellow birches that were not a bright yellow but a silvery yellow, and gray birches that sometimes were bent almost to the ground from the winter's snow.

And there were the elms left over from the nineteenth century when farmers had planted whips—slender, unbranched shoots of American elm—to domesticate and beautify the homestead. It was sad to see them—massive torsos that the seasons were breaking down bit by bit. The wood was gnarled and almost impossible to split. Occasionally we came upon them in the middle of what seemed like nowhere but wasn't—once a farmhouse had stood there. Sentinels, the elms had died on their watch. Nearby, weathered clapboards soft with decay lay on the ground along with the usual array of rusty pots, pans, and broken crockery. We stared up at the dead trees and down at the shards of lives. The massive, leafless stillness spoke to the wretched indifference of time. Their ruined dignity warned the encroaching woods that the arboreal world was a mere wink. Even the most stolid matter was corruptible. They were sculptures of loss.

When I looked at one of my familiars, such as the pine in back of our house that had grown up in a gigantic U-shape, two fifty-foot limbs rising from the trunk at around thirty feet, I considered the hazards of growth. Some impediment had caused this curious formation. The awkward tree kept growing as I kept on living. Habit had a sort of genius, yet it might take shapes that made the eye wince. I thought of the terrible ability of living creatures to adapt, to get along, to say the current regime is okay when the current regime is not okay. Eventually a windstorm would wreck those two unnatural limbs that had become trunks. The tree would have lived a reasonably long life, however. Like many people under many regimes, it had managed. Its awkwardness had not been ruinous; its inconvenience was silent.

The bark was surprisingly delicate, and the pitch was sticky. The fragrance was that thick, turpentine sweetness that is pine. I didn't have a problem understanding how people had once worshipped trees. Such barbarism, as the Judeo-Christian tradition termed it, signaled an awe and fondness I could sympathize with. The mental, omnipotent God in heaven I could not see had never moved me. Perhaps, as pantheists felt, God spoke through the trees. It seemed a pretty thought but an unnecessary one. I wasn't inclined to look further or deeper than what I saw and smelled and heard. If my senses were stupid and childlike, so be it. These great, leafy delusions were vulnerable, yet stalwart.

※

Poetry lives and dies in feelings, whereas science lives and dies in theorems, facts, hypotheses, and laws. In the twenty-first century there would be little argument as to which domain influences daily life more. Pharmaceuticals and technology both attest that we exist quite literally for science. What we eat and how we travel, communicate, attend to our bodies, and amuse ourselves—all indicate that the applications of science are not to be denied. Science is the inheritor of the indomitable, evolutionary impulse that brought life this far. Planetary time is vast and slow, but science plugs in the perspicacity of the dogged yet sprightly human mind that darts to an insight in a seeming second. Science testifies to the epic weave of blind, ceaseless diligence. Its gifts are plainly equivocal, but there is no turning back.

As for poetry, after the sporadic schoolroom encounters are over, it takes no particular effort to live one's life and forget that it even exists. In a city you might see a poem on a poster in a bus or subway car. You might hear a poem for two minutes on public radio. Or you might be traveling in a car and be listening to the contemporary rock station, the talk radio station, the classical station, or the news station, or be talking on a phone to someone about what time you will be getting home or which brand of tortilla chips you should buy. Poetry wants attentiveness, not distraction, and because it shows us pathways of emotion, it admonishes us that we can always feel more deeply. Such an admonition may be hard to hear in the world science has created.

Attempts to reconcile the two tend to soften their distinctive thrusts. Science is wary and incredulous and demands proof; poetry is spiritual and credulous and knows that feelings routinely dwarf their causes. Yet science, as it dutifully investigates what exists, manifests its own credulity. The scientist reports to the lab each assiduous day, a testimonial to the calm belief that matter will be around much as it was yesterday. Even uncertainty is a principle. Poetry, however, is episodic, haphazard, and incredulous—it honors the imagination that realizes that reality at any given juncture is a social hoax, that the elasticity of the human imagination is a glory and a horror. For poetry, each day is truly different. It honors the urgent pulse that can change in a moment and the turncoat heart that one second says one thing and a second later says the opposite. Poetry delights in surprise because its skepticism is founded in the turmoil of the senses. Despite its proud pedigree, it was born yesterday. It proves nothing and is forever making one-of-a-kind discoveries. Little wonder that it is easily dismissed as the ravings of subjectivity.

Technology famously gives us a sense of control; it harnesses material predictability, be it x-rays or radio waves or engines. Poetry, however, twists and turns as it focuses on what is, yet seeks to express the inexpressible. There is more to any moment than meets the eye, science knows that well. So, too, does poetry, but it has the temerity to delight in our unknowingness and vulnerability. Living in a house whose technologies were primitive felt like living inside a poem—we were creating a life that took its reasons for being not from the practical dispensations of science but from emotional impulses. We weren't disavowing science—how could we? We were, though, as we sought to feel the immediacy that resided in simple living, uninterested in its imperatives. The inquisitive excitement of modern times, the pageant of experiment, surmise, explanation, and invention, seemed to us beside the point. It wasn't a brilliantly red and orange winter sunrise or a gently raining, peeper-filled, spring evening where you could feel and hear the earth coming to life. It always came after the coaxing, vivid, riveting presence, a patient retainer cleaning up what beggared description in the first place.

The changing seasons form the crucible in which we experience time on earth. In their passages they reassure us and, despite the occasional ferocity of weather, sing an essential lullaby. I watch the trees shiver with rime frost in winter, leaf out and blossom in late spring, grow in the strength of their greenery in summer, and let go of their vigor in aptly named fall. I stare at the mute earth and kick the many leaves. I bend over to touch them. They are dry and crumble to my touch, or on a wet day they are slick with decay. I forget them as they become the soil beneath my feet, but the seasons keep reminding me of the permanence of change. The paradox of mutability is that it is timeless.

When, in my twenties, I first encountered the great Chinese poets such as Li Po, Tu Fu, and Wang Wei in various translations, I was captivated. I did not know such poetry existed. I am still captivated, for when I pull one of them down from my shelf I am in touch with the human seasons, the drama of people feeling their changing lives on earth. It is a poetry that is steeped in regret and momentary joy, in loneliness and celebration. It is a poetry that is founded on the image as an expressive genius in its own right. Declarative talk is dear to us but cheap. We can make assertions till the end of time, but they remain assertions—the moods of the will. The vanishing solidity of the Ten Thousand Things is another story and one that poetry's spirit wants to claim for itself. It can't, of course, but the recognition, the salute to how pungent and bittersweet mutability is, has made for some of the world's greatest poetry.

Poetry in Christian cultures often has groaned under the mighty burden of salvation. The poet is caught in the vise of trying to justify existence in the light of a judging eternity. The hunger for epiphany is understandable when one considers how great this pressure is. Because it seems to jettison some unbearable weight, the clarifying moment feels redemptive. Classic Chinese poetry seems content, at once, to accept and proffer the various gifts of existence as sufficient in themselves. Human vicissitude and waywardness are just that. Our lives are the patterned seasons, and our lives are the infinite, day-to-day, moment-to-moment variations within those seasons. Heaven can wait. We are feeling creatures whose lives on earth are precious.

The Road Washes Out in Spring

Consider Li Po's "Autumn Lines" in David Young's translation:

> Clean fall wind
> clear fall moon
>
> leaves heaped by the wind
> leaves scattered
>
> a cold raven
> flaps slowly
> from his roost
>
> thoughts of you
> fill my head
>
> will I ever
> see you again?
>
> the ache
> around my heart
> gets bigger

One marvelous facet of any poetry that comes from a deeply lived life is how each line in the poem offers a fresh perception. The longing in Li Po's poem is predictable, but the movement from stanza to stanza is profoundly vital. We feel in the beginning of the poem how the natural world is the natural world, neither good nor bad but only and truly existing. There is wind, a moon, the leaves in their various states, a bird. The precision of the language concerning the raven quietly thrills. We are left with a human being's wonder and ache. Then the poem is gone. There is no fuss, no trying to explain, no assertive mind tidying things up or trying to improve them.

Many of the Chinese poems I found in the translations of Arthur Waley, Kenneth Rexroth, David Young, Robert Payne, and numerous others offered such deeply unapologetic and genuine moments. In early June I watched the blossoms fall from the plum tree we had planted. What was I to do with their thin, white gracefulness, their delicate scent, and their perishing? The Chinese poets raised a grateful cup to such beauty. Both the cup and the beauty made life bearable. The resolute weight of have-a-nice-day happiness, that temporal glimmer of salvation, did not plague them. They were neither striving for some justification nor asserting one. They were free to feel the best, the worst, and the calmly middling. This freedom to feel was rooted in the endless marvel of being alive on earth. "What a show!" as the great Polish poet (and devotee of Asian poetry) Czeslaw Milosz exclaimed in one of his poems.

Li Po did not make one thing into another. He honored the life force, and he honored his own human woe. At the end of his poem "High in the Mountains, I Fail to Find the Wise Man" (again, translated by David Young), he sees a spring but does not find the wise man:

> a flying spring
> hangs a white plume
> from a jade-green peak
>
> he's gone, they don't know where
> I lean my grief
> on two or three pines
> and walk away

To make feeling so tangible must be why poetry exists. Any day that I went for a walk in the woods, I could feel the spectacle of mutability, a spectacle that at once dwarfs our works of art and lends them such poignancy. The Chinese poems I loved were tiny—that was part of their power. As my wife and I walked on an abandoned dirt road in the faltering afternoon light, I could see myself as a wayfarer, a cousin of Li Po's. "Who lives here?" I used to ask Janet when we came upon our isolated house that stood in the midst of so many trees. "Perhaps some hermit sage," she answered, and we laughed.

❧

The length of the road from our neighbors' farmhouse to our house measured almost exactly a half mile. It was, when we built the house, a discontinued road, which is to say a road that no one lived on anymore and was not maintained by the town. "Maintained" meant plowed and worked on to whatever degree was deemed sufficient by the de facto road commissioner to keep a road open for year-round driving. No one said that year-round driving on a gravel road was easy, only that it could, more or less, be done.

Our road ran first through a field with a distinct dip in it that required a culvert to channel the water. Because they often were not buried in the ground deeply enough, the metal culverts had a way of heaving with the frosts. In spring, the run-off flowing madly in the ditches and out of the woods would go under the culvert, the culvert would sink, the soil on both sides of the culvert would wash out, and a modest chasm would open up. This happened any number of times. Many an afternoon on the way back from work, I would pause before the culvert and ascertain whether or not I could get across. More than once we put two hardwood planks across a good-sized gap and drove our car across, Janet beckoning as to where to put the wheels, with me driving very, very slowly.

The field was actually the best part of the road. Most of it was flat, exposed to the sun, and dried out reasonably quickly in the spring. From the field the road headed uphill and was bordered by trees. On the upper part of the road steep banks stood on both sides. Anyone who has ever examined a road has noted that the road wants to be above rather than below its banks. Alas, our road was never going to reach such heights. In addition, the last two hundred or so yards of the road went up a modest hill. The hill was shaded by large pines and some years did not thaw out until late April or early May. When it did, holes would open up that made driving a distinct challenge. More than once we buried a wheel in mud over the top of the tire. Stanton, our old neighbor who prophesied that we, as know-nothing hippies, would never last more than a year or two "up there in the woods," would come along with his pre–World War II tractor, attach a chain to our front bumper, and pull us out. He would make an understated remark about the road ("this road ever see daylight?") and smile a resigned smile. He lived on the level portion of the road that didn't wash out, fall in, or buckle.

I never knew how alive the earth was until we had to deal with the road up to our house. In winter the road was plowed, and because the ground froze, we didn't have to worry about getting stuck in mud. It did, however, ice over and lead to sudden lurches on the drive downhill. I became adept at veering and then correcting that veer while keeping up a conversation with my wife. On the uphill drive, it led to the great question, "Can we get up the hill?" If the answer was "no"—and it was sometimes—then it meant backing down the road, a head twisting, literal pain-in-the neck process. Frequently, getting up the hill meant gunning the Subaru while in first gear and frantically wiggling to the right and the left as the car staggered and whined. Since the driveway into our house represented a slight incline, the driver had to regain enough control and momentum after cresting the hill to make it around the corner of the driveway and up into the driveway itself. When my steering attempts failed, I wound up parking the car in a cleared area on the other side of the road. Because that area was the turnaround for the plow truck, I couldn't stay there but would have to get into the driveway before the next snowstorm. When the plow came along, it blocked the mouth of the driveway with packed snow, but that was nothing to take personally. It was The Way of the Plow.

Winter was a cakewalk compared to spring. Washouts from rain left deep runnels. The road collapsed in some places, creating formidable sinkholes. I realized that the word "abyss" was not simply a metaphor. Sucking, swampy mud covered areas where the ditch and the road were indistinguishable. We often left the car at the beginning of our portion of the road and walked the half mile. I remember Janet and I carrying a futon (a clumsy thing that is hard to get a purchase on) up the road in a rainstorm. Every step felt like ten. Being educated and young, we compared ourselves to characters in a play by Brecht—Mother and Father Courage. We carried laundry, groceries, children, lumber—you name it.

On clear days in the spring we could be seen throwing stones into holes in an attempt to give the road some foundation. It was peaceful, satisfying work chucking those stones in. I could imagine how the farmers had chosen each stone to make the walls that ran everywhere and that had once designated boundaries and enclosed the fields that were now woods. They had taken what was at hand; though New England didn't have much topsoil, it had plenty of stones. A stone wasn't going anywhere. The splat or kerchunk it made when we dropped it was pleasing.

Our endeavor no doubt would have seemed crazy to most people who had better things to do. Yet the road, in all its ingloriousness, was our necessity. We came to understand how roads were named for the families that had lived on them. They existed for human purposes and were, in their changes from season to season, not too-distant members of the family. They were of the earth, and they had their moods. As we shored our road up, cleaned the ditches, and dug around the culverts, we were crafting it.

You didn't, by and large, craft a road, however. It wasn't mac-ramé. You brought in heavy machines and bulldozed to make a ditch or spread some gravel or put in a new culvert. The town did what it could. We weren't a high priority; there was no reason we should have been. The so-called main roads in town often were so badly rutted during mud season as to be barely passable. Nine miles an hour would have been a sane maximum speed. As you sedately bounced along, you could feel your vehicle's shock absorbers giving up the hydraulic ghost. We had, after all, chosen to live on what had been a discontinued road. That was our affair.

And it was. Driving the last mile on a summer's night with the windows down and the rich, warm, earthy air pouring in was sub-lime. The lights would be out in our nearest neighbors' farmhouse. Stanton and Ella were asleep by nine o'clock. As we headed up to-ward our place, the saplings on the side of the road almost grazed the car. A fox might dart across or, more often, a skunk or porcu-pine would be briskly waddling off to one side. "Where are we going?" we used to say to ourselves and to our children as we drove past the last electric pole into the darkness where no one seemed to live. Playfulness and wonder were in our voices. "Where are we going?"

Our landing in rural Maine was part of a historical moment that was known more or less as the Back-to-the-Land Movement. The capital letters seem somewhat ridiculous since there was no or-ganized movement, only a demographically tiny number of people who felt the same vibration emanating from the 1960s, namely, to abandon the metallic hubbub of urban life and try to live with the earth. Although we were only in our twenties, we had already had our fill of the galvanism that was trumpeted by the tireless word "new." It seemed no accident that America had been heralded in Europe as the "New World." If the scene in the movie *The Graduate* where Dustin Hoffman is given one word of sage advice—"plastics"—spoke for that New World's contribution to what was once called "civilization," we wanted no part of it. The economy we wanted to practice, however effaced it seemed, was a long-standing, handmade one. *The Whole Earth Catalog*, that oversized compendium of practical, esoteric, and funky lore, was its printed portal.

We reaped a serious amount of scorn for our actions. Our parents informed us that we were throwing away our educations, if not our lives, by going off to live on a dirt road. They had labored to get ahead in this country. They had put together savings accounts over decades and learned to play the stock market and invest in properties so that they could take vacations, buy big cars, and send their children to college. They had believed that each generation materially improved on the previous one. As we indulged a useless fantasy and rejected what they had striven to create, we were going backward. In their calculating yet optimistic eyes, we were spoiled, callow youths who had read too many books, seen too many movies, and had far too many romantic notions.

Their viewpoint made good sense. We attempted to put a positive face on our actions, stressing that rural life would improve our characters and make us stronger people. It didn't fly with our parents. They had not been born yesterday; they knew that we were pursuing an unofficial and not ballyhooed (though basic) American freedom—the freedom to go off and, from the point of view of happiness as the pursuit of what money can buy, screw up. We were hopelessly existential when, according to our parents, we should have been pointedly economic. Money bought comfort, security, and leisure, all of which helped to avoid pain, an avoidance that constituted, according to that sage of happiness Thomas Jefferson, "the art of life." Individual desire meshed neatly with public opinion— "I want this, too!" The national genius was perennial novelty. As in Las Vegas (the nation's alternative capital), anyone with the cash could buy in.

The Road Washes Out in Spring

Living in a house in the woods that lacked the bare amenities was another story, one that had more to do with the pursuit of old realities than with glossy happiness. We figured that, since everyone was busy getting ahead, there was room for us to stay behind to savor the breeze and go blackberry picking. One less car on the freeway wouldn't be noticed. Amid the whirlwind of modern, abstract energy, there was room for some people to work hard at simple endeavors.

Our way of life meant among other things that, until our daughter reached the threshold of adolescence and balked at the indignity of it, we didn't have a telephone. When I filled out a vital information form at work and left the space blank where it asked for your phone number, the secretaries were polite but baffled. "That means you don't have a phone, Baron?" "That's right. I don't have a phone." Pause. "Okay," in a very uncertain tone of voice. Everyone had a phone. Why would a person not want a phone? I dressed conservatively, drove to work in a car (rather than coming by horseback), did my job conscientiously, but no phone? Was I on a most wanted list?

Now and then we called our parents, siblings, and friends from a pay phone outside the general store in the next town. We wrote letters. We savored the stillness. The sounds in the house were modest ones—a window closing, a match being struck, a fire whooshing in the stove, a pump sucking up water. We had nothing against anyone. We loved some people dearly. We didn't want, however, the jangling intrusion. In turn, we were told we were selfish; we were thinking only of ourselves. Probably we were. What communications came to us were communications we wanted to come to us. We had decamped in order to live deliberately. Why choose distraction when living on the earth was the sweetest experience?

We hadn't rejected everything the United States offered—far from it. Europeanized America was the place you ran off to. Once there, you were free to start running off again in pursuit of whatever gimcrack scheme or notion inspired you. Like many thousands who lit out for the territory, we were seekers who were fleeing. That we didn't know what awaited us was part of the charm. We had heard rumors and read stories—elsewhere existed. Our parents shook their heads ruefully. They had wanted their children to be thoroughly American. Alas, we were.

⁂

Max had been big in the sixties. The Vietnam War was his war. He didn't fight in it; he resisted it. He counseled draft resisters, he spoke at rallies, he signed petitions, he marched, and he went to jail. His name had been in many a newspaper article; his picture had appeared on a fair number of front pages. He had a handsome, craggy, big face with thin but long white hair. His smile was toothy and energetic. He may not have been charismatic, but he had plenty of chutzpah. He wasn't bashful in front of a microphone. He had been on the side of the objecting angels and had reveled in it.

As the sixties deliquesced into the puddle of another decade and as the war wound down and was declared over as far as American officials were concerned, that spotlight ceased to shine. Max existed in opposition to the immoral status quo and was a formidable opponent. When he lacked a specific cause, he always had the government to rail at. The government, however, wasn't listening anymore. It wasn't war times, mimeographed-manifesto times, run-off-to-Canada times, frag-the-lieutenant times, take-it-to-the-streets times. Max hated to feel that his phone wasn't being tapped. Although Watergate provided a welcome, vengeful pleasure, it, too, was over. It was back to the spectacles of Superbowls and oligarchs, celebrity writ stupidly and lavishly large. Henry Kissinger smiled for the cameras. The "common man" (in Max's phrase) looked on and applauded.

Circumstance had brought Max to a ramshackle farmhouse on a country road in a town much like ours, where the denizens tried to make frayed ends meet, hurrying over the frost heaves and ruts in not-so-new cars and trucks. The townspeople were out buying the necessities—Budweiser, milk, hamburger pizza. They were taking their kids to Little League games, the babysitter's, and K-Mart. Some went to church on Sunday—many did not. I never saw Max mingle with the locals, although he had been an organizer back in the city. Most of these people had supported the war, and some of them had served. Some had lost family members and buddies. They weren't interested in Max's take on what should have been. They had been doused by what was.

Their indifference didn't seem to faze Max. He existed in the mental universe of permanent leftism. According to Max, even the blindest of the rural working class would see the light some bright, unfailing day; Central America would come to central Maine. Various redolent whiffs of Marxism had made their way into his system while he was growing up in the Bronx and while he pursued degrees at several large state universities. He had done the theoretical spadework in the I-Like-Ike fifties and was ready for action when the freewheeling sixties began to happen. His chief delight lay in explicating the idiocy of politicians and their pathetic, greedy, lying machinations. A contemptuous, half-amused smile played on his face when he lacerated the likes of Lyndon Johnson. Johnson wasn't his equal; Johnson was child's play. Though Max could grind up any political reputation pretty quickly, he masticated for decades.

Despite his lack of interest in the hardworking locals, Max believed devoutly in the genius of radical democracy. What that constituted depended on which day of the week you talked with him. Typically it was a compound of Tom Paine, W. E. B. DuBois, Engels, Eugene Debs, Spanish Civil War anarchism, Herbert Marcuse, and the folkways that gravitated around ethical culture, ethnic food, and a subscription to *The Nation*. I never knew what Max and his family lived on. Neither he nor his wife had a day job. Only after his death did I hear what I had suspected—a trust fund kept him afloat. Despite his anguish about capitalism's unfairness, it did okay by him. I'm sure he would have been indignant if I had called him a hypocrite. The money was his due. Wall Street owed it to him for opposing Wall Street.

During the last decades of his life, he must have wondered at times who he was abetting. He had a large correspondence with other righteous old lefties, but his sphere of political influence had shrunken woefully. I sat in the farmhouse's kitchen on a Saturday morning, drank peppermint tea, and listened to Max rant about the fascists who ran the United States. He occasionally emerged from the genius of his words to see me idly staring out the window at the trees. I wasn't much of a convert. Life, I felt, was fluky, and people were mysterious. Any kind of true belief made me uneasy. I figured that mostly people wanted to get laid and have enough money in the checking account to make the rent—assuming they had a checking account. I didn't understand the attraction of ideology. People liked to drive around in cars; that's what the United States seemed to be largely about. It wasn't Athenian democracy, but the human race had done a lot worse, too. Max thought I was pathetic, but someone's ear was better than no ear at all.

I liked to bait him. I would say, "Now, Max, I think I know my history. Wasn't a fascist someone who followed Mussolini or Hitler? How can you use that word with any accuracy about Ronald Reagan? I don't like him either, but a 'fascist'?" Max would look at me with scorn and pity. I didn't get a lot of things. I didn't get power. I didn't get the wisdom of socialism. I didn't get big lies. My ignorance went on and on, a prairie of naiveté. Ravens lighted in trees and flew off in search of carrion. I asked for an oatmeal and raisin cookie. Max's adorable son wandered through the kitchen in search of a Parcheesi board he had mislaid. His wife walked in from her painting studio and asked if he was up for lentil stew for dinner. Off in a corner, Mitzi the old Labrador slept contentedly. Max was explaining how Gorbachev was reinventing communism. How did Max know what was happening in the Kremlin? His hectoring voice felt out of place in that placid, domestic environment. What a terrible, beautiful, ludicrous world it was.

I didn't go over often. Since I was never going to get with Max's program, there wasn't much point to it. I was rising at six a.m. each morning and driving to my job in a mill town whose fondest hope was that it could remain a mill town, while Max rearranged the tea leaves of history. I liked it best when I got Max off the rhetoric (though he didn't think it was rhetoric) and into the byways of memory. I liked to hear what Berkeley had been like in 1952 or Ann Arbor in 1956. It sounded pretty swell. A lot of miserable materialist knowingness hadn't dawned on people yet. Entertainment hadn't taken gigantic bites out of art. Correctness hadn't paralyzed inquiry. Max talked about sharing a jug of wine, listening to Leadbelly, Stravinsky, and Django, and arguing about Sartre and Camus. The young were reading serious books and were going to make a better world. I didn't blame them or him. I was trying to do the same thing.

When I got him back to that era, Max looked wistful. His face took on a rare sense of introspection. His eyes, which usually gleamed with a verve that seemed almost fanatical, were sad. He suspected that in the interval, despite his efforts, some idealism had died. Perhaps that was why we were all living in the country and intent on growing string beans and strawberries. We had to prove life for ourselves. We had to touch the famous green fuse and reinvent ourselves accordingly. Still, Max's vitality bridled. "But what about now?" he would ask me of the nation that basked complacently in the Hollywood president's amiable glow. The dreams of the sixties that had felt like such buoyant, powerful realities seemed a hundred years ago. Beyond asking for another cup of tea and that wonderful wildflower honey that Max got from an old woman down the road who kept bees, I had nothing to say. We were L.I.A.—Lost in America.

❧

Our house was heated entirely with wood. That meant a fireplace that was mostly for aesthetic purposes, a large cast-iron box stove in the main part of the house, a cook stove in the kitchen area, and a small box stove in the ell where our children's bedrooms were. Keeping warm was our constant responsibility. No turning a thermostat up or down, no going away for two weeks or even two days in the winter, no phoning the heating oil company to schedule a delivery. It meant deliberate work throughout the year: cutting trees down, limbing them, hauling them out, cutting stove-length wood (three different lengths for the three different stoves), splitting the lengths by hand, wheeling those pieces to one of the two woodsheds I had erected, stacking them, and—finally—carrying each log or stick into the house to fill the wood boxes. Staying warm was a work ethic unto itself.

To me that labor was a species of bliss. It wasn't that at times I didn't get plop-down-and-not-budge tired, or that my eyes weren't stung on a summer day by prickly sweat, or that my fingers weren't numbed while lugging wood on a January morning, or that a hard-to-start chainsaw didn't tick me off. It was work, however, that was directly connected to our well-being. It was work that made sense in the most basic way—you do this, and you get that. It was work that instructed you and comforted you. For some moments on earth I knew what I was about.

Every step of the process had its own rhythm and intensity. The first task was what was called "cruising"—ambling around in search of hardwoods that could be thinned for firewood. Typically these were red maples, a common and fast-growing tree that gave off a tolerable but not particularly impressive amount of heat. Sometimes they were beeches that were starting to get soft in the center or gray birches that had been done in by winter. We didn't burn anything like oak (famous for giving off regal amounts of heat) because our land didn't have any oaks of any real size. They were coming back, however. I saw them here and there and wondered at the mysterious process of forestation. The largest oak was a half mile down the road in front of Stanton's farmhouse. Perhaps the thin young oaks I saw here and there had come from it.

I learned to see the woods as discrete trees. I probably spent more time contemplating how certain trees had grown up in certain places than I did thinking about what needed to be cut down. Some areas would be all one type of tree—a tall, shady grove of hemlocks, for instance, that brought to mind my father's poetic first name, Sylvan. Others would be a riot of competing trees—red maple, striped maple, white birch, gray birch, yellow birch, beech, pine, balsam fir, spruce, hornbeam, poplar, tamarack. "Mixed woods" was the apposite phrase. The fecundity and randomness of what grew up where made me understand how people thought there was something called "Nature," a capitalized force that could not be denied.

It was a concept, but a credible one. Many times I thought back to grade school and the leaves and seeds I had pressed into a scrapbook for a school project. As a child I had marveled at how various they were. How dreary and forbidding the earth must have been when it was a cosmic puddle! How fortunate we were to live here after such an unfathomable splurge of years! Why wasn't human life built upon gratitude or at least some degree of humility? How was it that God created time? Wasn't it the other way around?

Felling trees invariably brought time to my mind. You could see the trees' years in their stature. Having grown up in a large city, I didn't know there was such a thing as a chainsaw until I moved to rural Maine. At first, the saw frightened me; a degree of which never went away. Caleb was fond of displaying the missing tips of two fingers on his right hand. "Got a mite careless one afternoon, Red, with a Homelite." The saw's power was signaled by its hellacious, ravening shriek. Yet when it was running well, the noise came to sound almost dulcet to me—a small engine doing its indomitable work.

Learning to fell trees was a trial and error experience. The errors hung up on other trees and didn't fall to earth. Or my saw got caught in the cut I was making, and I would have to pry it out. Or the tree didn't fall where I wanted it to fall and crushed some trees I didn't want to crush. With each tree, I cut a notch, made the back cut, set in a hardwood wedge or two, drove them into the cut with an ax head, and watched for that second when the tree began to teeter and groan. I stood back or sometimes pushed a bit, and over it went— a crashing plummet so mighty that the tree often bounced when it hit the earth. After I turned off the screaming saw, the silence was uncanny. I was elated from the intensity of the work, relieved, yet shaky, too. The elemental power of the experience, the drama and fierceness, was scary. It never became second nature to me.

Once, men had felled trees with axes and saws, and though the gasoline engine changed that, the work remained daunting. I have never understood the logic of economics, because to me the people who work in the most dangerous professions should be paid the most. The woodcutter in rural Maine is at the mercy of more forces than can be counted. His body is, in the scheme of things, dispensable, yet it's the only one he has. He has to keep heavy machinery running efficiently, and he has to be willing to work on days when most people would much rather be inside. He has to deal with the fluctuations of the wood pulp market and insurance costs. Considering the labor involved, what he makes is a pittance. Yet I never heard one of them complain in any serious way. This was where they grew up, and this is what they did. Many of my high school students couldn't wait to get into the woods. It was a man's work; the decisions a man made each moment counted hugely. As an occasional front-page article in the local paper demonstrated, men died for their mistakes in the woods. That risk was one thing that made you feel so alive when you were cutting down trees. As Hayden Carruth put it in his poem "Regarding Chainsaws," it "makes you know you're living."

I sawed off the limbs of the felled trees and made a pile of the larger ones. I'd cut them up eventually into short lengths that we'd burn in the cook stove. I spread the smaller limbs on the ground so that the coming winter's snow would start to flatten them. Given enough winters, and they would break down and become duff. I sawed the trunk of the tree into four-foot lengths that I stacked with the help of a pulp hook. My next job was to get those lengths from wherever I was in the woods to the area adjacent to our woodsheds.

During the first few years of our life in the woods, the area where I cut was close enough to the house so that I could balance a four-foot length or two in a wheelbarrow and wheel it to my pile. Given, among other things, the roots, dips, ruts, and tangles of shrubs, it wasn't a smooth journey. "Arduous" would have been more like it, but I never wanted to back down from work. It was my guide and could teach me unwanted yet helpful lessons, such as patience and perseverance: a log falls off the wheelbarrow, you put it back in. Over time, however, the distances became prohibitive. I had to find other ways to bring in the wood.

Whenever woodcutters were lumbering nearby, I asked them to come over. I worked with whatever they were using to bring wood to the road—tractors, horses, and, a couple of times, oxen. The oxen were not like anything I had ever encountered. It wasn't only that they were such massive yet mild creatures, it was their strength. I would load up a long trailer bed that consisted of two metal beams welded to two old truck axles and fill it with four-foot hardwood lengths. The pair of yoked oxen pulled steadily ahead. Their faces betrayed no signs of exertion. The man who owned the team walked beside them, occasionally swinging a switch of fir to guide them. When, as sometimes happened, some lengths fell off, the oxen halted and waited. One sensed that they could stand there all day if they had to. As often happened in the woods, the world of minutes and hours seemed to have been swallowed whole.

To work with the oxen and horses was a blessing, and the men who used them were different from the men who used the big machines known as skidders. They weren't using animals because they despised machines. After all, they had to transport the creatures in a trailer hitched to a pickup, to say nothing of the pulp truck with its cherry picker that loaded what they had cut. It was because, both economically and emotionally, animals made sense to them. "You can't talk to a machine," one man told me who had a team of horses and who did some cutting on our land. He qualified it: "You can but you'd be a damn fool." He laughed. The horses René worked with were like extensions of his own body. The simplest call and gesture elicited an immediate response. They were workhorses—thick and sturdy and powerful—but they moved beautifully together. One sensed the pleasure they took in doing the work for which they had been bred.

René took every occasion to praise his team. The work he did and they did was strenuous, but the horses gave it a constant, lively grace. They were living animals, not automatons, and thus, to a degree, unpredictable. They ate, shat, pulled, got tired, whinnied, and nuzzled each other. They were his confederates in being alive. For all their strength, they were the thin pulse of consecutive moments. He couldn't work them without thinking about them and how they felt. Why would he? His pace fit with their pace. The fact that most men preferred machines to horses was understandable, because men nowadays hadn't grown up with horses. René had. There was an uncommon gentleness in him. He smiled and laughed during the course of the day and paused to notice a blue jay's flight or some tracks in the snow. He lingered when the horses got a scent and took an exaggerated sniff himself. "If I was only half as smart as they are," he mused.

The wood that I brought in had to be cut to the proper length and then split. I split everything with an ax or a long-handled splitting maul and a metal wedge. It was satisfying work. I could have rented a gas-powered splitter and split a winter's wood in a few weekends, but that would have taken the joy out of it. I could work at my own speed for as long as I felt like working. I wasn't bound to anything beyond my own body as I gauged where to place a wedge or as the maul's blow divided the wood in a clean split. I had to keep ahead in these endeavors so that the wood had time to dry; because it was full of sap, green wood burnt poorly. Winter never left my mind, but that seemed as it should be. It was the essence of the North Country; its inevitability was consoling. We lived in the implacable embrace of the seasons; we would stay warm despite that and because of that.

And stay warm we did. Although we had our share of chilly moments when we rose on a winter morning and the temperature inside the house had plunged, most of the time we were toasty. On those cold mornings we hopped around while joking about the invigoration of it all as we put together the newspaper and kindling and started a fire in the 1920s cook stove that stood in the kitchen. Heat was soon radiating from the small firebox. There was nothing quite as comforting as those first glints of warmth off the black stovetop.

When I hefted a piece of wood before putting it into a stove, I could tell that wood's history—when I had cut it, where and how I had taken it out of the woods, and how long it had been in the woodshed. What was impersonal—a tree—felt personal. Then it became heat that turned to ashes that—come spring—we threw on the gardens or the grass around the house. Each stick of maple, birch, ash, beech, and even the aspen that burned up like a matchstick seemed a requisite gift. The warmth we felt on a wintry night was earned. The sucking hum of the stove fire was a song.

※

One ancient saying about poetry asserts that its subject is always poetry, that every poem is an *ars poetica* of sorts. As sayings go, it is a reasonable one. Poetry seeks to create some semblance of beauty in a small place and is inevitably self-regarding. Intent on its means, poetry must mesh the meanings of words, their sounds, and the rhythms that words create with one another. A reader (if not a writer) may feel that with prose one can cut three yards of the stuff from a bolt and it will be serviceable. There is no such cutting for poetry. It has to be wrought; even the woolliest poet is a formalist. How the words go down on the page matters hugely.

The counterbalance to the formalist urge is the goad of subject matter. Though there have been poets, notably Wallace Stevens, who majestically seem to have dispensed with that goad, for most poets it has been crucial. One remarkable aspect of American poetry in the latter half of the twentieth century was the growth of subject matter. What was not written about began to be written about, often with a vengeance. A strong case could be made that the main topic of American poetry—with Robert Lowell and Sylvia Plath firing the first salvos—became the nuclear family in all its dysfunctional glory. Also, women started writing about taboo topics that hitherto had largely been outside poetry's genteel purview, beginning with the facts of female anatomy and moving into the harrowing dynamics and outcomes of sexual abuse. At a less intense pitch, poets reveled in poetry's ability to engage the mundane. Poems appeared about every possible scene from a life—spreading jam on a piece of toast, buying a used car, or remembering the time in fourth grade when someone threw up in the cloak room. In addition, people from diverse ethnic backgrounds started making their presence strongly felt in American poetry. That was all to the democratic good.

What I, amid the trees of Somerset County, wasn't so sure about was the personalism of American poetry, how almost inevitably whatever was being written about was filtered through the lens of the self. The American self has a big appetite. For better and worse, the society is constructed around that declarative, consuming, identity-sprouting presence. Where it ends and the rough world of the non-self begins is a hazardous guess. The notion of things and events existing in their own right seemed dubious in the light of many a poem's automatic self-involvement. A journalist acquaintance of mine who took a dim view of contemporary poetry once told me that poets might give the pronoun "I" a holiday. It wasn't so much the "I" that offended as the notion that the "I" is at the center of whatever universe exists (rather like the pre-Copernican universe where the earth was at the center). Had the gods died for this?

Such a personalism preferred the mantra that the personal was the political, that the poet's situation was a sum rather than an integer. The personal seemed equivalent with the responsive anecdote—where I was when Kennedy was shot, when the Berlin Wall came down, etc. "What's it to me?" was the question the personal was bound to ask and more or less answer. For all its sincerity, that approach seemed reductive and flimsy. A fiction writer would delve into the world behind and around Kennedy's assassination; a poet registered the effect of the assassination on his or her own life. It made sense that the nexus of each life was how each individual experienced life, but whether that nexus constituted the whole of poetry's ambition was another story.

Some days in the United States it feels as though the intensity and sincerity of the individual viewpoint is more than enough. There is such an incredible diversity of human beings that there always is something to be learned from encountering an authentic instance of that diversity. Other days, however, the primacy of the individual viewpoint feels like convenience—a well-meaning conceit that affirms how all roads lead to the self. The focus on the self may seem so strong that the public domain barely exists. It occurred to me more than once that American personalism showed how poetry was dwarfed precisely in the way that the apocalyptic weapons and unbelievable machines that humankind had invented dwarfed humanity at large. Perhaps the dread and awe that humankind felt for its products militated against the foundational awe of poetry—the miracle of our being alive on earth. The staggering breadth of modern times, its proliferation on all fronts, from the trivial—endless, witless entertainment—to the ghastly—genocide—made poetry seem like a small fist clutching a bit of crumpled paper. Who could gauge how much electrified numbness had crept into our collective lives?

I knew my life in the woods wasn't an escape from anything; I remained a member of that mass, media-saturated, commerce-driven society that promoted the wealth of narrow choices. What spooked me was the feeling that the assertions on the part of the self, however well-meaning or right-minded, were born of indulgence. What spooked me was the feeling that there was nothing real beyond the yacking, anecdotal self. I had the uneasy feeling that the eagerness to testify to the spark of the individual life resided in that life's need to convince itself of its vitality. If it didn't, it might fall into despair and impotence. Yet egotism, however kindly, eager, and liberal, did not seem a better fate.

I understood the self's distaste for engaging subject matter in its own right. It seemed to call for little more than the lethargy of description, that troweling of language that smugly or simplemindedly believes that being dutiful to externals can make art. It seemed to put the self on the outside looking in. It seemed to put reins on the imperatives of the imagination. At its worst, it smacked of those wooden apostrophes to "Death" and "Hope" that the nineteenth century was big on. And yet, didn't what existed have to be honored for its consequential, independent actuality? And wasn't a lived life as it encountered foreign matters crucial to being a writer? Didn't the famous shock of the Other depend on the writer getting outside the self and its agendas?

One day an evangelical minister came to school and informed me that the library shouldn't have books such as the play about Helen Keller and Annie Sullivan entitled *The Miracle Worker*, because only God could create miracles. However much I may have wanted to, I couldn't conjure him away. I did tell him about the commitment that libraries had to the First Amendment and that readers had their rights. He scowled, nodded, and told me I would be hearing from him soon. I never did, though his manner (overbearing and anxious at the same time), his person (lean as if there were not an ounce of pleasure in him), and his clothes (faded white shirt buttoned at the collar and black pants to go with black shoes) stayed with me. Perhaps he was making a point; perhaps a member of his congregation had been upset about the book (of all books to be upset about!); perhaps he was sounding me out. I was from the great Land of Away and my values, no doubt, were poisonous. In any case, his presence registered a simple fact—his religiosity had its own notions of what should and shouldn't be. I didn't so much wonder about my response as I wondered who he was. Over the years, I met various students who went to his church, and I learned more. What I considered intolerance was for him the virtue of strict belief. The only words that mattered were God's. Literature was superfluous and blasphemous.

Occasionally I heard from acquaintances who lived in distant academic enclaves. They didn't consider those environs enclaves. On the contrary, they were at the hub of whatever the self-regarding Zeitgeist was divining. They sent more interviews with poets and articles about poets to me than actual poems. I wondered about the American propensity always to be looking for the next hot product. I wondered about the amnesia that went with that looking, the automatic interest that went with the word "contemporary." Over time we stopped writing one another. They had their careers. My bringing in another load of maple logs didn't seem at the hub of anything.

Poetry depends on the honesty of sensibility, but sensibility isn't especially inclined to truth telling. As it showcases its perceptions, sensibility prefers embroidery, the comforting filigree of self-involvement. Language, particularly as it is embodied in poems, can be a very marvelous cocoon. Texture soothes, whereas encounter, the sheer bumping into the obdurate that characterizes drama, can be perilous. And perhaps that was where I had strayed as I encountered the world of deer rifles, skidders, scripture quotations, mud, and coffee brandy. One mild spring afternoon, I stood dazed and shaken beside my car after a pulp truck driver fell asleep at the wheel and his eighteen-wheeler careened down a hill toward me, then veered to the other side of the road, and, before coming to rest in a pasture, took out a couple of telephone poles as if they were toys. I breathed out deeply with relief for myself and for the driver (a twenty-year-old who was intact though abashed), but I exhaled, too, for the magnitude of everything outside my little mental sphere, for the vast web of stubborn yet unpredictable realities. They claimed me more than I could claim them.

*

Our neighbors, Stanton and Ella, lived in the same farmhouse in which Stanton had been born not long after the turn of the twentieth century. As a married couple, they had never moved away from that house and had witnessed the twentieth century from the splintery, gray-with-weather boards of their front porch. It looked out on an oak tree that Ella had planted from an acorn, a dirt road, and a field that had been indifferent pasture at best. They had cows for decades, but as Stanton was quick to point out, "the government forced us out with their rules and regulations." After World War II, when those regulations started to take effect, the state wanted milking machines, cement floors, and refrigerated tanks. Stanton made enough to get along in a bare, country way. He had no money for improvements. Going to a bank and asking for a loan would have been unheard of. Stanton sold off the herd and went to work in a sawmill.

It was hard to believe there was a twentieth century when one entered their world. Rising before dawn they started a fire in the cook stove to heat the kitchen and make their pot of coffee. Stanton sat in a rocker and did the word jumble in the local paper. Stinting though he was with words, he liked puzzling them out. Ella wrote out her day's menus on a letter-sized tablet. She made three meals a day. They were solid country meals—biscuits, meat, gravy, vegetables that Ella had canned, pies, and cookies. Nothing was made from mixes or any similar, modern corner-cutter. When they went out to eat, it was a very special occasion. Even then, as Ella was quick to insist, a restaurant could never touch home cooking. According to the season, they worked around their place: stacking wood, tending the garden (Stanton liked to hoe), cleaning, repairing whatever needed to be repaired. Stanton remembered the old times when the seasonal tasks were more communal—cutting ice, for instance. That had been a long time ago.

When we arrived, Stanton and Ella were in their early seventies. They were opposites. Stanton was glum New England. He treasured adversity, and though life had not given him an unusual dose, it provided enough to keep him cranky. He delighted in blame. Usually the government (which meant the state—the federal government was far beyond his ken) was the recipient of his outbursts, though it could be environmentalists and other worthless do-gooders who had banned what Stanton considered to be helpful pesticides like DDT. Most of the time, Stanton kept his opinions to himself and was content to remark that a good day was bound to give way to a bad one or that the winters were not as severe as they used to be. A two-day blizzard was his delight. He was lame from an accident he never spoke of. Perhaps life had given him an unusual dose.

Ella was cheerful, day in and day out. It wasn't that her life was easy. Money was always tight; Stanton had to have been a difficult person to live with—ornery and at times downright perverse. Ella was smarter than he was, also, and for her to defer to him had to have been an ordeal. She was a genius at gentle wheedling. "Don't you think?" she would ask Stanton in her girlish voice. She would smile her cutest smile (she had dimples), and you could feel Stanton, wooden as he was, melt. This comedy went on into their eighties— Ella the tease, and Stanton the flinty but good heart.

Chores were Ella's passion. She baked most days—muffins, breads, pies, cakes, cookies. The hard work the two of them did— even in their old age—seemed to burn off the calories they consumed religiously. Ella cooked everything from scratch (as did we) and shook her head at the world of meals in boxes and frozen packages. "That's not food for people," she would say. The very notion of the microwave horrified her. She canned everything she could get her hands on—string beans, peaches, beets—and had a whole battery of recipes for preserves, relishes, and pickles. Going into Ella's cupboard was like stepping back into the nineteenth century. A woman was someone who knew how to feed her family on her own. Ella seemed happiest wearing an apron.

She loved to clean their modest but neat house. Each day (except for Sunday) she dusted, wiped, and swept. She literally whistled while she worked. Folk tunes like "Oh Susannah" were her specialty. The bandana she wore around her hair when she was cleaning highlighted her pleasure. The house and certain areas of the land around it—the strawberry patch, the gladiola bed, the semi-circle near the porch where hollyhocks came up each year—were her domains. When she was digging in the gardens, Ella would put on Stanton's overalls. Otherwise, she wore a dress. Women didn't wear pants.

Emotionally, it's hard to imagine two people more different from myself and my wife than Stanton and Ella. They were circumspect, cautious, and narrow in the way country people can become narrow. They knew what they knew and didn't want to know any more than that. Call it ignorance or call it a kind of wisdom. In any case, they visited us three times in over twenty years, and we lived a half mile apart. We were at their place constantly—paying visits, helping out (they both had hip operations and were laid up at times), asking questions. They never asked us about ourselves or what we were doing up there in the woods or how we felt about anything. Feelings seemed to be the farthest thing from their minds. They were representatives of that New England way of life that cherished privacy and would never dream of presuming on others or about others. They were upright, circumscribed people.

A hardscrabble life makes for a hardscrabble soul. Stanton and Ella had the consolations of their Methodist religion, and those were considerable. Ella sang in the choir, and they went to the little church in the village every Sunday. They both believed in heaven in a calm, almost practical way. Ella liked to gossip harmlessly about the minister—the suit he had on or his haircut. The church's suppers comprised a large part of their social world. Occasionally a relative would pay a call, or they would go visiting Ella's relatives who lived forty miles to the south, or "down country" as Stanton put it. Again, it all seemed as though the nineteenth century had never passed. When you sat on their rickety front porch among the numerous cats Ella kept (and whose kittens Stanton drowned in their pond) and the geraniums that she had potted in Maxwell House coffee cans, you were taking your ease on that yeoman's farmstead Jefferson had treasured. It was a vision that was a backbreaking pipe dream. It was a vision that left the engines of capital to do their work as they saw fit. Still, it was peaceful to sit there and chat about the old days with the two of them—when they walked miles to school or how the snow covered the tops of the telephone poles one winter. The cats sparred with one another or dozed. Ella noted that a chair was about to give way if Stanton didn't fix it "right soon." No one was going anywhere. It was sweet.

We were in love with the country, and Ella and Stanton must have known that because they softened over the years. They still kept their distance (never once responding to our repeated invitations to see our beautiful flower gardens), but they knew we worked hard. They respected anyone who did a day's work. They knew we had survived difficulties—chimney fires and ice dams on the roof and going without water. On that count, the strangeness we evinced—we definitely weren't Christians, for instance—was forgivable. They were never what anyone would call warm. They were used to a world where each person had to take care of him or herself or bear the consequences. Emerson's self-reliance wasn't a notion to them; it was reality. They were used to a world where economically things did nothing but get worse, where the ambitious and the curious moved away. One of their sons lived in Arizona, and the other in Alabama. The therapeutic, bare-it-all mindset of modern times was literally unbelievable to them. They would look at the television, and Ella would say, "Whatever are those people doing?" Then she would get up to stir something on the stove or look out the window at the chickadees. Stanton would fetch some wood. Life went by like a profound dumb show.

The two of them were pillars of a world that had collapsed long ago. It didn't deter them. Engines of rural purpose, they did what they needed to do. Stanton, who often seemed nothing as much as bewildered, complained dryly. Ella, the sunny wife, provided good news about small things—a two-for-one sale, a cardinal that appeared that morning at the bird feeder. They both sensed that the nation whose flag they cherished had left them behind. The glamour purveyed on television had nothing to do with them. Their indefatigably wholesome ways didn't count for much beyond a politician's hypocritical salute to America's farm families. The cows along with the laborers who helped get the hay in, the water troughs and cornfields, all that designated a farm had gone. Their barn was a museum of implements.

They had never tried to get ahead. Ella, as a farm wife, never worked at a paying job a day in her life. They were conservatives—people who want to hold onto a way of life that suited them. They endured; they persevered. They attended closely to what they had. Stanton knew he counted for little in the American scheme of things. Given his reticence, he must have been a hard, remote man to have for a father. It seemed no accident that his sons lived far from the homestead on which they had grown up. Stanton had never improved his poorly drained fields nor cared to thin his dense woods by selectively cutting. Something dark was stuck inside him and never left. There were people in town who considered Ella stuck-up and self-righteous, a woman who was too good for those who occasionally needed to raise some hard-drinking hell. They both were teetotalers.

Their lives were earth-bound. The century of unimaginable horrors, of Hiroshima and Auschwitz, of the Gulag Archipelago and the Khmer Rouge, passed while Stanton and Ella lived on that spot where the south sun came through the oak tree, where they watched generations of squirrels and foxes and meadowlarks come and go. It was theirs, and in their Yankee way they treasured it. Ella even wrote poems, rhyming couplets about birds and trees and one about a porcupine that had taken up residence in their falling-down barn and that Stanton eventually shot. It never would have occurred to them to praise us to our faces for the work we did on our place and for how we brought up our children. Life was a series of chores.

You did them or you didn't, but you certainly didn't talk about it. To romanticize Stanton and Ella would have been absurd; they were cloistered, chary people. To deny them their dignity would have been glib; they were at one with the ground beneath their feet. They never made a fuss about it—or anything.

❊

Our plumbing was rudimentary. We had a pitcher pump in the kitchen that was hooked up to the dug well and that drained into a cement block dry well. A valve at the well end of the line kept it primed. A few brisk pumps gave us modest gouts of cold, clean water. In the bathroom we had a large wooden tub that we used as a shower stall. We'd fill a black plastic bag with water, then use the small nozzle at the end of the bag to shower ourselves. We learned what most of the world already knew—it didn't take much water to get clean. The wooden tub also drained into the dry well. Such was our plumbing.

All of which is one way of saying that we had an outhouse. Every time we had to defecate, we made a trip outside. We did have, as an amenity of sorts, a portable toilet (a more or less up-to-date chamber pot) that we used for urinating. The bottom part of it was detachable; we dumped it once a week or so in the outhouse. With its prominent handle, Janet and I joked that this was the closest to an attaché case we were going to get. Otherwise, it was a trip to the outer world. Nature called.

When people contemplated the way we lived, the outhouse was what stopped them. Wood heat was bearable, the lack of a refrigerator was a bother but bearable, but an outhouse was intolerable. Even a pleasantly appointed outhouse like ours, a two-seater with screened windows that offered a view of the piney woods that sloped down to the road, an outhouse that stood at the end of a winding path lined with ferns and striped maples, was still an indignity. Even an outhouse with a sizable overhang to keep off the weather and a toilet paper holder that consisted of a nail on the back wall that was high enough to deter mice from nesting in the roll was still an outhouse.

The Road Washes Out in Spring

Even an outhouse that displayed a laminated invitation to a *Paris Review* cocktail party and that contained a bucket of lime to throw on what was gathering below and kill off any offensive odors was still an outhouse. "What about January?" people would ask. You could feel the dread in their voices.

January was January—you didn't want to be constipated. As a whole grains sort of family, we rarely were. Still, it was cold. Wearing gloves to take a shit was always a bit strange. My member felt that drawing-into-itself numbness that was reminiscent of an early June plunge into a lake that had only lost its winter ice in late April. It wasn't, however, the end of any world. No one got pneumonia. No one died in the outhouse. We were putting ourselves back into the earth. If no one cared to contemplate that, it was understandable. Shit isn't at the top of the list of conversation topics. Our waste is furtive and execrable. We know the face that we prepare for ourselves when we return from the bathroom to a group of people. "I was talking to a man about buying a horse. . . ."

I grew to like the outhouse experience, mostly because every day I was reminded of how close to the earth I was and how the natural world was always there. Despite the extra steps, the donning of outerwear, and the variety of weather, it was comforting. In the middle of the night I walked out with a flashlight and felt the night woods bustling around me. I had been sleeping, but the raccoons weren't. Often I stopped on my way (if I wasn't heeding an urgent imperative) to admire the night sky. The sheer sprawl of it made me feel as though I were seeing it for the first time. Since there was no light pollution in the country, I could see every distant iota the naked eye could observe. I breathed in the air, be it dank or cold, soft or humid. Whatever my head had been cranking about (usually some form of worry) lapsed. I fell into a large, internal silence.

There might be dew underfoot, or mud, snow, ice, matted leaves, or dry earth. I might be walking out in boots or sneakers, mudders or sandals. It might be raining, snowing, blowing, or quite still. It wasn't a long walk, but I might see a toad or frog, salamander or green snake. Inevitably some spider would have taken up residence in the outhouse itself. And the daylight view from the outhouse was marvelous. I could contemplate the trees; they were alive but seemed to be doing nothing. They were there—I couldn't get enough of that there-ness. For a few moments, I was off in a pure space with nothing to do (reading was impractical given the lack of light) but contemplate. When, after doing my business (a favorite euphemism), I closed and hooked the outhouse door, I was still outside. "All this never stops going on," I would think to myself. That the natural world was not the episodic stuff of my consciousness was a small insight, but one it took me a long time to get.

It wasn't as though we already didn't spend many hours outside. We did. The house with its many windows (six on the south side of the main part of the house) was an invitation to the out of doors. The trips to the outhouse were a humble reminder that the cycles in our bodies were echoes of the cycles around us. Despite my less-than-transcendental purpose, a mysticism came over me; the world around me was within me as much as I was within the world around me. As I sat in the quiet of any time of day or night, I heard only that quiet and my fundament's unrepentant sounds. Those squeals and bleats passed, leaving in their wake the quiet and my relieved body. As the spiders testified, the quiet was alive. As was I—a natural man.

A country life teaches how consequential our endeavors are. Cut the wood an inch too long, and it won't fit into the stove. Don't cover the tomato plants, and the frost will get them. Bury the wire fence around the garden good and deep, or the woodchucks will dig it up. This feeling for consequences can be oppressive; picking up every stitch can wear a heart down. It's not that you can't laze in the sun on your granite door stoop and admire the deep July sky. It's that the habit of attentiveness doesn't flag, nor does the feeling that if attention isn't given, some hell will have to be paid. In our county there were house fires every winter that typically were caused by a wood stove that was a bit too close to a wall or a chimney that wasn't tiled properly. Looking at the charred remains of someone's home gave any person pause. I had a student who died in such a fire.

Rural people are famously handy because they grow up paying attention to a thousand small things. More than one guy I knew could build a house (including chimneys), plumb it, sheetrock it, wire it, install the hot water heater, and then step outside to fix anything that had wheels. In Ella's generation, a woman could quilt, sew, knit, bake, cook, can, garden, doctor, and a host of other verbs. Not that long ago, the country economy had been more about barter and self-sufficiency than it was about money. Banks were a necessary indignity but no place you would want to make a habit of frequenting. Whenever I ran into Caleb at the local bank, he hailed me as if I were a fellow convict: "I guess they got you, too, Red." Money wasn't what life was about. It was pretty low on the list actually.

What haunted me was the bleak determinism that a sense of the consequential could enforce. The awareness of how one thing led to another could be stark; part of the lore of the older people around us centered on families and how traits were passed down from unhappy generation to unhappy generation. The countryside we lived in was sparsely populated. More people had lived in our town a hundred years ago than lived there now. Although there was plenty of space, there was little anonymity. Everyone knew about everyone else, and that, too, was an attentiveness, though an unwanted one. Usually when a sentence began with "Her mother was like that," or "His father acted that way," the rest of what was imparted was not congenial. Feelings festered.

The dread that informed Edith Wharton's *Ethan Frome* or the poems of Edwin Arlington Robinson started to make sense to me. The woods enclosed the people. The admirable practicality of rural life didn't make for psychological insight. Urban life with its crowded, peopled din encouraged speculation, but the country encouraged acceptance tempered by watchfulness. This was, as a person came to pay careful attention to the tracks that animals left or where birds nested, endlessly fascinating. Yet I couldn't help but wonder about the human endeavor. I could feel people around me staggering beneath the weight of the solitude, to say nothing of trying to get by.

A friend of mine used to joke that there were three groups of people in a small town: alcoholics, recovering alcoholics, and people who ministered to alcoholics and recovering alcoholics. It was, of course, no joke. Until I moved to the country I really didn't know what the bottle was. Guys in college had partied and then on Sunday night or Monday morning gone back to their schoolwork. This wasn't partying. It was the comfort of numbness, the sentinel of false cheer, and the shallow shout of bravado. It was predictable and grim, and it spelled, almost inevitably, a shutting down that frightened me, a clenched stare at a familiar despair. It was an endurance contest, the resolute wages of self-destruction.

I stood by the cooler at the local store buying an occasional six-pack that lasted for a week or two. I looked around me and saw guys I knew (and sometimes their wives whom I knew less well, if at all) buying the six-pack or twelve-pack for an evening's drinking along with the whiskey and brandy to chase it. We nodded and smiled briefly. For the moment we were fellow congregants. They got into their pickups and drove off. Mostly they got home in one piece, though the local paper was routinely headlined with stories about cars going into telephone poles, off embankments, or into other cars.

The inner life, such as it is, in go-get-'em America revolves around individual striving. Desire and anxiety make for powerful goads. In the country, however, there isn't much to strive for. You are living on earth—getting your wood in, going deer hunting every fall, at the end of summer putting the garden to bed. It's the over and over of life that's beautiful but monotonous. The tonic of social novelty—new cuisine, new movie, new fashion, newly gentrified neighborhood—comes thirdhand in the form of a video release or a chain store opening up in a nearby town. Cherishing the wheel of what happens again and again, what will never be hyped because there is no money in hyping it, takes some imaginative work. Once upon a time there had been organizations like the Grange that did cherish rural life. Once upon a time there had been farms and all the rituals that went with them, but that way of life was attenuated. People worked in mills and small, fluorescent offices, drove trucks, minded the neighbors' children at daycare places, or got along as jacks-of-all-trades. It wasn't a land of farms anymore, but it wasn't anything urban either.

Sometimes I paused outside the store and talked about the weather, the shape the roads were in, one of the Boston sports teams, or how we were doing "up there in the woods." It was that time between getting off from work and going home for the evening. The parking lot in which we stood constituted the chief public space in our town, a town so small it lacked its own post office. It might be winter and already had been dark for a while. No one seemed to bother with meteorologists in sports jackets making weather forecasts on television. If you lived here, you watched the sky that hovered over the endless trees. We might talk about the sunset—not its ragged or ethereal beauty but what the clouds might indicate. Some nights you could taste the air and feel the snow coming—a tiny, precise, metal weight on your tongue. I was a stranger in the country who was trying to learn and who was learning. More than a few of the men and women getting into their trucks already knew too much.

⁂

Poetry is like a plant. It wants to grow toward the sun of spirit and vision. Those two are, immemorially, the sustainers and ends of poetry. It isn't that poetry seeks to transcend the human—far from it. Poetry is the human confronting and celebrating itself as it aspires toward what can't be fully said but can be fully felt. It is freelance spirit; it is its own blessing.

Vision is the grounding of feeling in the habits of timelessness. It is the vibration, the aura that hovers above and around and within each earthly moment. Poetry feels that emanation and seeks to articulate it. It is an impossible task, hence the deep, beckoning charm of poetry. Hence, also, the steep hill poetry represents to any writer. To denominate an experience in lines is one thing. To make the reader feel (since poetry is an art of embodiment) the vibration of

63

authenticity and that vibration's inevitable extinction is very hard. That it has been done time and again is an impressive index of human accomplishment.

The great issue for poetry in any era is how much it believes in its task. The distractions are numerous. Poetry can be socialized and lose its way trying to please (or repel) others. Poetry can become complacent about what constitutes its art and mistake a rut for a trampoline into the empyrean. Poetry can self-consciously push its means to the exclusion of feeling. Poetry can become a forum for the ego and believe that sheer amplitude of voice is sufficient. Poetry can strike attitudes. Poetry can believe that sincerity is art or that being dutiful is a virtue. Poetry can confuse intensity of subject matter with accomplished feeling. Poetry can pretend that spirit and vision no longer matter. Poetry can traffic in higher obfuscations. No wonder so very little of what we write is going to last.

All this doesn't deter poets, nor should it. Human energy will have its way. The distractions and debilities, however, aren't bad things for the poet to keep in mind. They are honest reminders of how the simplest looking of all arts—"I can write a few lines down and call it poetry"—remains the hardest of arts. Words weren't meant to do what poetry wants to do with them. Words are counters we use in daily life to note whatever we wish to note. We exchange them and live more or less unconsciously with them. We blurt them out when we stub a toe or receive another bill in the mail; they serve well enough in giving vent to importunate sensations and feelings. They are odd compounds of practicality and oblivion that human usage saves and buries at the same time. To celebrate them in their own right yet suborn them to whatever emotional errands one has undertaken in writing a poem is a delicate task. It's very easy to err on one side or another: to make of language an idol or to treat it as so much agreeable stuff from which poems can be readily fashioned.

Perhaps that's the greatest of the paradoxes. Poets aren't, in their inevitable sensitivities, notably well-balanced people, yet they are called upon to practice an art that takes a great deal of balance. Passion, if it is going to be fully articulate, demands equanimity. Shakespeare, the man who stepped outside of himself, remains the arch poet in this sense. How he summoned up all those characters and resonant lines is a testament to ardor and obsession, but a testament to distance, too. He gave voice to a staggering array of human feelings yet was able to walk away from them. It was only writing. That seems blasphemous but isn't, for at its outer limits (*King Lear,* for instance, or Dickinson's most harrowing lyrics), poetry so indulges the power of the poet that the poet's personality, that bundle of opinions and history each of us treasures, is beside the point. Identity is straw for the fire of language. In that sense the degree to which the poet believes in the medium of his or her art is mystical—but not quite. A certain stubborn materiality remains in the lines and stanzas, a good shred of sanity that has moored some very troubled souls and that the seemingly untroubled Shakespeare was able to take to the nth degree. Light as the words seem, they aren't airy.

It is a measure of how aberrant the 1960s were that so many took the words of Henry David Thoreau to heart. The words of Thoreau, of course, are meant to be taken to heart. He didn't write to be analyzed. He didn't write to please any fashion or lead any school. He was the purest sort of egoist—the one who holds each moment of his life in great esteem. A wry altruist, he wished that others might hold their lives in great esteem, not according to the dictates of attainment but to the conscientious thrill of being alive. Thoreau, like his fellow American Walt Whitman, spent a goodly amount of time avoiding the justifications of an all-consuming job. The American enterprise of transmuting anxiety into the cult of work, the wearisome afflatus of Protestant justification as it sought (and still seeks) to find an ethic in timeserving, never attracted Thoreau. Walking around on the earth and noticing what was happening were plenty enough. Mere observation kept him employed; curiosity delighted him.

The initial, incantatory sentence, however many times I read it, remains thrilling: "I went to the woods because I wished to live deliberately, to front only the essential facts of life, and see if I could not learn what it had to teach, and not, when I came to die, discover that I had not lived." The woods? Why not foreign travel or political ambition or philandering? The woods? What did trees have to teach anyone? What did living simply (rudely to any mildly polished soul) have to teach anyone? The whole purpose of America was to rise in one's station, not go live in a cabin and dine on dried apples and unleavened bread. Wasn't Thoreau foolish? Immature? Unimaginative? Indifferent to sex, power, greed, and all that makes the world go madly round?

Thoreau's character has never been the point. The point is the experience. Do you dare to take his dare? Do you dare to accept the sufficiency of the earth? Do you dare to live with the night and the sunrise, the shade of trees at noon, the rain—pelting like anger or soft as poppy petals—and the solitary quiet? Above all, the quiet, for the quiet cannot be borne by most people. It savors of emptiness and idleness; it makes people nervous. Nothing is happening. How are we to know that we are alive in the midst of silence? To verify our vitality, we need a tumult of some sort. We need to proclaim the genius of our fidgeting. We need the reassurance of noise, even if it is only our voices avoiding the terrors of insight.

In truth, the woods weren't utterly quiet—there were birds and winds and squirrels and sounds one might not have thought of before. Trees boomed in the shattering cold of January, pond ice groaned as it stretched and contracted, tree frogs gave recitals throughout the warm months. The earth was ever vital. It was the people who lived on the earth that were problematic as they mistook their individual purposes for life itself. Thoreau wished to reside with the wholeness of life on earth. The distractions of humankind were just that. Everything, as it existed in any kind of weather, fit quite comfortably in nature's back pocket. People were the ones who were forever squirming.

But wasn't deliberateness tedious? How many fires did one have to start to learn what heat was? How many mornings did one have to rise with the sun? How many evenings did one have to lie in bed and do nothing but listen for the owls? Nature was all repetition, whereas humanity thrived on novelty. Wasn't novelty the spark of humankind? Even Thoreau liked to go on trips and see other rivers, lakes, and forests.

The deliberateness that Thoreau sought was as variable as the weather. That was its pervasive joy. Great, almost unspeakable pleasure lies in frank attentiveness, the awareness that the ways of matter hold infinite treasures. Transience makes those treasures all the more piquant. The churning human mind is the measure of nothing but its own excitement and lethargy. It never created a tree swallow or a March gale or a bed of pine needles. I say this not to produce paroxysms of abasement but to speak to the enduring savor of being alive in the natural world. The question wasn't what Thoreau was doing in that cabin. The question, apropos his famous night in jail, was, what was everyone else doing by not living in that cabin?

He knew the answer too well. Sometimes one feels he is taking out his bemused frustrations on those hardworking farmers of Concord he loved to mock. How mulish and shortsighted they were. Yet how well they slept at night, sure as they were of their labors and account books. Buddhism warns us against making things, of replacing what is with concepts of what is. Thoreau wished to feel what life was like when it was stripped down to satisfactions that needed no catalog or touting. Squishing a just-picked, sun-warmed raspberry on one's tongue or jumping into a pond on an August afternoon needed no advertising or explication. The inclination is close to Buddhism's. We know at various moments how sweet a drink of water can be. There it is. What if we cherished that sweetness? What if that cherishing became a principle of our existence? What if our living were a meditation?

Thoreau realized that he was turning his life into a totem of sorts. It amused him. Despite the seriousness of the man, a whimsy remains in him. He was alive to the humor of any human endeavor, and his own seriousness is meliorated by that humor. This wasn't the often oppressive joking of Americans seeking to establish a degree of civility amid the welter of so many different people. It was the froth of free will. For a time he chose to live at Walden deliberately, but he also chose to tramp most days around the environs of Concord, and where he paused and where he turned were the markings of that free will. He followed his rather beak-like nose. His example was his own life; he required no others (so unlike Emerson!), but that example could translate into any life.

I like to think of his steps on the earth—springy, zigzagging, steady, pensive, sturdy, halting. I like to think of him squatting and examining the corpse of a vole or shrew, listening to the rush of a snow-melt stream, watching clouds or feeling the wind on his bare arms, breathing in the mysterious night air, fingering the leaf mold beneath an old tree, or bracing himself in the quick, morning cold. I like to think of him as sweating and shivering and lolling and even occasionally scratching himself. He stood for the opportunity the republic presents almost in spite of itself—the chance to walk un-hindered by the manacles of opinion and to feel what there is to feel in any natural moment. Perhaps, given the flightiness of the human mind, such a disposition is unnatural, but often when I was outside our house and stood still on that bit of earth I felt that the "essential facts" were not recondite, yet more than I could ever comprehend. Life in the woods humbled and exhilarated me, for I began to feel how much there was to be alive to. I had Thoreau, in part, to thank for that.

⁂

If there is such a thing as a mutable eternity, it is snow falling in the woods. I am thinking of a windless, steady plummeting. Nothing is moving except for snowflakes. You can hear the snow faintly ticking on the pine needle branches. You can hear it descending—a soft sift of air. You are held in the hand of something enormous yet gentle, something extraordinary yet calming, something evanescent yet quite palpable (from a Latin word meaning "to touch gently"). Every surface receives the snow in its way. A large, fallen, curled maple leaf collects the snow in its center. A boulder's stored heat resists the snow at first, then its surface turns wet as if it were raining, and then, with un-boulderlike delicacy, a thin frizz accumulates. On top of the garden gate a fragile white skein begins to perch. Little, almost derby-like hats grow on the garden fence posts.

The Road Washes Out in Spring

The mown grass around the house fills in gradually. The stiff, frozen blades seem like little heights. Then the snow, as it mounts, receives itself. Another landscape is created, and for months we live in that landscape.

Snow is fanciful, and dour New England has always been of two minds about it. Scenes of snow-covered fields and ponds filled with skaters and children careering down hills on sleds are part of the region's lore, but it is hard to clutch something cold to one's heart. Winter is death's trial. Its shadow is daunting, its weight at once tranquil and bothersome, as a person slowly climbs a ladder to rake snow off the roof and slowly climbs back down or takes off mittens to dry by the wood stove and then puts them back on. Steadfast motions become lengthy rituals. Some, as the chiropractors can testify, start to feel quite painful. Yet the routines retain a dreamlike quality. Didn't I just take my boots off? My feet feel so much lighter without them, but they also feel snug and confidently weighty with them on. Load after load of snow goes onto the banks that line our driveway and beside the paths we shovel to the house, to the woodshed, to the outhouse, to the propane tanks. When the snow is light and dry, I feel as though I am moving feathers. When it is heavy with water, I am slinging wet cement.

The rhythm of the work is lulling and blissfully stupid. Anyone can do this, and everyone did until the advent of machines. Caleb always had someone come in a pickup truck to plow his driveway. Shoveling wasn't a self-respecting man's work. He would rather have stamped a path between his driveway and house than wield a snow shovel. Stanton had a snow blower that one of his sons had bought for him and that he treasured. He wasn't another weary bumpkin moving snow with a shovel. He had a machine that roared happily, smoked busily, and threw the snow a considerable distance. It was broken most of the time, but that was part of the pleasure as far as Stanton was concerned. He could complain about the snow (while secretly relishing the adversity) and about the snow blower (while enjoying his status as a machine owner and hence a genuine American). It was the best of both aggrieved worlds.

For decades we shoveled. It was part of the experience, and we were fools for experience. It had its taxing moments, as when the town plow came by at five in the morning and plugged up the driveway with a solid, three-foot, white wall that I had to shovel out to drive to my job. It was more work than I cared to do at six o'clock on a very cold morning, but it reminded me once again that I was living on earth and not in some ever-convenient mental scenario. When Stanton talked about the times when people dug out the roads in blizzards that stopped the plows, I shook my head and marveled. It had to be done and they—men, women, and children—had done it.

The wonderland landscape that the snow created was part of a false eternity. For some months the ground disappeared and was replaced by a fantastic sculpture, at once shifting and static, decreasing and growing. We looked out the window and stared dreamily at the indifference of timelessness. Snow was philosophy made tangible; its solidity was empty. It asserted evanescence, yet as long as the temperature stayed below freezing it wasn't moving, nor, plenty of days, were we. We kept the fires going in the stoves, cooked our meals, read books, and strapped on wooden snowshoes to go walking in the woods. The snowshoes made webbed patterns that joined the tracks of weasels, hares, deer, and mice. We were there, too, lumbering along, the less-than-graceful, enthusiastic humans.

The snow world was enchanting. We, who had moved to the woods, in part, to be enchanted, were particularly susceptible. We wanted to merge with the natural world, to fall into it and revel in our descent. We wanted to be the snow, to surrender our tiresome, declaiming egos and experience utter stillness. That yearning was fanciful but balanced by hardheaded labor. The wood didn't cut itself; the paths didn't shovel themselves. We were romantics with backaches.

The gift of snow was the shiver of wonder. Being out in the late afternoon when snow was coming down thickly and the stillness total was pure, meditative magic. Even the children could touch—for once—the sky. By extending a hand, we felt an airiness that had broken into innumerable fragments and descended to earth. How strange it was, yet comforting—a legend in which we were living.

There were no distractions, no signs, no lights. The earth itself had disappeared. It was disorienting in the way that legend is disorienting. Surely, there were never such things as headless horsemen or talking cats, yet in an impressionable mood one can believe in them. Our workaday minds lapsed. The drift of thoughtless eternity clung to our coats, hats, and gloves. We exhaled and saw our staunch, white breath. We stuck out our tongues and felt the cold dissolve on our warmth. As humans, we, too, were legends—an incredible surmise made credible. This beauty would have to be pushed aside, but that was later, always later.

Most weekday mornings and afternoons in fall, winter, and spring I drove to and from work through the small town of Norridgewock, Maine. Norridgewock was the sort of town one drove through (it is on the main east-west road of northern New England) and didn't notice anything to speak of. Three major roads went through it, along with the railroad and the Kennebec River. As a crossroads, people had gathered there. Though like any town in the United States it had its boosters, it was a town that deserved the prefix "un," as in unlovely, unprepossessing, unremarkable. There was a lawyer's office, a restaurant (breakfast and lunch), a Laundromat bathed day and night in sickly fluorescent light, a couple of markets, an insurance agent whose plate glass window was occasionally broken in the middle of the night by some adolescent full of anger and liquor, a public school, and a Seventh Day Adventist school. There were three garages, one of which also sold cars. For a short while there was a porn shop called The Little Beaver. For a number of years there was a bakery whose owner made perfectly fried doughnuts. For something like forever there was an establishment that was a combination general store, pool hall, and luncheonette. It was more like something down south than up north. It closed though, one unremarkable day. Times changed, even in Norridgewock.

Most houses were in calm states of decline. People had other things to do with what money they had than put it into clapboards and paint. More often than not, they aspired to vinyl siding, which promised no upkeep costs and possessed the demented lure of technological perfection. Get-with-it practicality overruled tradition time and again. Caleb, who could be commonsensical to a fault, became dyspeptic when the topic of vinyl siding came up. "Wood's not good enough for people, Red, they shouldn't live in this state. That stuff is ugly."

On a little island of ground in front of the post office there was an obelisk that honored the Civil War dead. The figure on the obelisk recalled Robert Lowell's "wasp-waisted" Union soldier in the great poem "For the Union Dead." He "dozed" and "mused," to recall two of Lowell's verbs. Although I was temperamentally prone to muse over that obelisk and the sacrifices that it represented, I realized I was in a very small minority. When I asked students about it, they inevitably replied, "What's an obelisk? There's an obelisk in Norridgewock? Right in town?" To those who read fantasy books the word smacked of the basilisk.

Those same students would go to war in Vietnam and the Gulf without hesitation. They didn't want the burdens of history (who in the land of possibility did?), but they were eager in their patriotism to take on new ones. The long view I favored was repugnant to them. They were young; the notion of remembrance was a mystery and an irritation. The past was an intangible land of imagination. Although photographs and movies were aids, it took the subtlety of words to conjure its many-sided perplexity. Even then its emanations were indistinct; it was, at once, more and less than a spectacle. Who knew what it was like for that seventeen-year-old from Norridgewock who died at Gettysburg? Why would one want to know?

To me it seemed that everything hinged on wanting to know, that the whole endeavor of calling the disparate country a nation fell apart if there wasn't some shared consideration of what people had been through. Because Americans are such a diverse people and there is no one set of historical ancestors, this shared understanding was hard. Part of the challenge lay in considering how incredibly various these ancestors were. Even those (and they were countless) who would have winced, to say nothing of scowled or spat, at the word "Jew" were my American ancestors. As a people, we needed to envision some sense of the past for many very different people. Without that imagining, we were without dignity and lived at the mercy of slogans and exhortations. Without that imagining, we had no sustained, empathetic discourse. Nor could the bland assertion of facts ever replace the weaving of imagination. Poets knew that. Jane Kenyon's magnificent "Gettysburg: July 1, 1863" enshrined that imagination as it presented a nameless young man ("hardly more / than a boy") dying on the battlefield. I drove back and forth to work, and year by year the obelisk seemed to diminish.

A factory near the Kennebec anchored the town. It was, in the parlance of Maine, a "shoe shop." Sneakers were assembled there. It was skilled work and busy work; many of the people had been at it for decades. The factory (a nightmare experience to me, who could do nothing in a timed setting) was a rackety, clattering home. It was steady work in which there was pride to be taken. Everyone knew everyone else there, as well as who needed a ride to work on a given morning, whose car was running and whose wasn't, who took two sugars in their coffee and who took half-and-half. In what was considered a fair bargain, the employees lived to service the machines. Without the operator, the machine was nothing; the operator treated the machine with the respect due the means of one's livelihood. I, who assumed degradation at the drop of a time card, regarded such labor from the other side of a great divide.

When people looked back at the culture of the factories and mills, it was usually with nostalgia. The world needed what the mill made; the mill workers took pride in that fame. The New England mills that were built beside the rivers are long, massive brick buildings that symbolized the strength of manufacturing, as if to say that this was one endeavor that wasn't going away. The endeavors, of course, did go away; it's painful to drive through New England and see the empty mills with their broken windows staring disconsolately at the indifferent rivers. The solidity of manufacturing is a hard thing to give up. That so many of a certain article could be made and then

73

cease to be made—no more wooden sleds, cordovans, clothespins, or blankets—boggles the credulous human spirit. That spirit craves over the course of its modest number of decades a degree of continuity, but in modern times the disruptive inventiveness of change is much stronger. Though the shoe, chair, or hat seems a totem of some sort, its magic has been compromised by its availability. It lives to be used and discarded. At best, it may be restyled; at worst, it may go out of date. Its value is perishable. That makes blunt, economic sense; yet, when a mill shut down, people felt as though the ground beneath them had shifted. It had.

On a winter's morning the shoe factory would be bright with electric light in the cold darkness. My car headed slowly over the narrow, 1920s concrete bridge that spanned the Kennebec and began climbing the hill that rose on the other shore. The river would be frozen. All that was flowing and easy was bound up in a stolid truculence. The town quickly disappeared in favor of fields that were turning into pine woods. I was heading north, and it felt like it.

On my way home in what remained of the winter afternoon, I looked again at the old farmhouse near the middle of town where the owners kept horses on their front lawn, or at the stark Grange Hall that every several months offered that homeliest of dishes—a boiled dinner. The day's work done, the parking lot beside the shoe factory stood empty. When I stopped by the post office, I chatted with the postmistress or waited my turn while a retired mill hand aired an opinion. She shook her head wisely and squinted into the dying brilliance that seeped through a large picture window. People were going to do it all over again tomorrow. Any educated so-and-so who criticized them didn't understand how hard they were trying.

※

One of the stories that I told myself was about the trees. They lived slowly; they moved slowly; they grew slowly. Their moments were long ones. They were impassive but susceptible. Most of what happened to them couldn't be watched or known. How they lived with one another was obscure but important. Together, they added up to a mind-defying number. Singly, they were quiet ministers. They spoke to one another in voices that distended language until sounds became lost on the outskirts of time.

Though it pleased me, this story was not the only one. I also needed the large, human story, the one that told however cursorily what hurly-burly, helter-skelter, hocus-pocus people were doing in the world at large. Having grown up with newspapers (the *Baltimore Sun*, to be specific), I needed the neat, foldable facade of the front page. I hadn't moved to the woods to escape what was going on in the world. I moved to the woods to think twice and breathe deeply. The news that I sought in the woods was of long duration; the news I sought in poetry was the power of moments. The newspaper, with its inveterate structure (as in the *New York Times*), reminded me how much that was deemed important lay in between.

The layout of the front page possessed a methodical charm. In the far right column, the Most Important Thing happened. Some days were quieter than others; the font size and length of the headline reflected how important the Most Important Thing was. It could have been a decision by the United States government to do something. Perhaps another nation was complaining about something, or two nations were wrangling—or fighting. Perhaps the American president had made some pronouncement. Perhaps it was an event that was more individual—an important criminal (a war crimes perpetrator or spy, perhaps) was being detained, tried, or extradited. Then again, the criminal could have drifted over to the far left column of the front page—a prominent story on the way out. In the middle of the page were miscellaneous important stories—a money story of some sort (because money is always important), a story about trends (scientific, demographic, or more frivolous), a story about the environment, a story about some health issue, or a story about some political figure who had seized the main chance or miscalculated. There could be a story about the leader of one of the political parties accusing the other political party of chicanery. Down at the bottom of the page (less important) would be an article about something happening in some other part of the world. Also, there would be an article dealing with something fetchingly human—a personal story about a farmer, tugboat captain, or school teacher, some regular soul to whom something somewhat remarkable occurred. Maybe long-lost sisters discovered each other, or someone's father appeared after empty decades. Or it could be more prosaic—maybe a single mom was losing her job. There would be a photo of her sitting at her kitchen table with an understandably glum look on her face. Together, the articles added up to a sum, however skewed and formulaic, that equaled the socialized world.

As I sat by the wavering kerosene light, I pondered this grid of experiences, virtually all of which occurred far from my rural door. The columns testified that events made a degree of sense. Despite the duress it purveyed, to say nothing of carnage, the newspaper was a time-out for someone like me who beheld a heaping measure of suffering each day. Some of the suffering I witnessed was the routine unhappiness of adolescence, that strangling, isolating, often angry self-consciousness, but some of it was barely masked despair and depression that was traceable to abuse. A guidance counselor once told me that, at any given time, we had three or four young women in our school (which was a small school) who had reported incest. Then there were gay students who were trying to survive in a small town environment in which the word "faggot" was as common as chewing gum. Then there were the teenage alcoholics, car crashes, suicides, farm accidents, and hunting accidents. I walked slowly up the walk to the local funeral home far too many times.

The woods presented me with a different sort of happenstance. One seed took, but another didn't. One animal lived, but another didn't. One tree thrived, while another stood gaunt and near dead. To this seeming randomness, the newspaper proposed the ant-like actions of human beings. We were ever industrious. We never stopped travailing. We slipped and fell, but some of us got up. We were always moving and giving off light and energy as we did so. We rarely shut up. Instead, we speechified, debated, decreed, refused, objected, concurred. No matter the time of year, we were throwing a ball. The dark senselessness of human actions didn't disappear; it was a rare front page that didn't feature a war, insurrection, or ideological murder of some sort. I knew I was not definitively safe; I, the reader, was part of the confused yet elated human parade. I ate some more popcorn and sipped the tangy apple cider a neighbor had pressed.

That the events changed from day to day was reassuring. All I had to do was keep living, and new things would keep happening. The Old World, the pre-modern world, had revolved around stories that happened again and again. Human beings needed reassurance about how they came to be here and why things happened the way they did. They needed to heed the stories that hid in the natural and supernatural worlds. I needed those stories, too. That was one impulse behind my seeking out the company of the trees, stars, and snow.

The charm of the modern world that the newspaper purveyed was its relentless, purposeful energy. You could argue that it was a stupid sort of purpose, that dynamism had nothing to do with feeling and thought, and I wouldn't disagree. Nonetheless, the story of endless change was satisfying because I would never get to the bottom of it. Ulysses made it to the end of the known world. The primal mind recognizes boundaries and respects them. I was a modern person and more hopelessly blithe. Even when staring at catastrophe—genocide, natural disasters, plagues, atomic weapons—I remained engaged, hence, blithe. I believed this whirligig would go on for something like forever. Science would make new discoveries. Countries would revolt, go to war, and even perish. People would pursue their strange, indomitable ways in nooks and corners of the planet and tell their stories to journalists. Change abolished change. There was a deep, awful permanence to human doings. I crumpled up the paper to start fires in the cook stove each morning. Often I paused to read an article and consider someone's picture—a somber refugee, a judge, a smiling ballplayer. These were people I never would meet but whom I obscurely knew.

The mild and objective prose belied the considerable time it took to write these articles. The writing portrayed a commendable steadiness, a refusal to give in to railing, grievance, and imprecation. All was as it should be, even when it wasn't. However volatile circumstances might be, the human tone remained considerate. The throbbing, poetic voice of grief, anger, dismay, and lonely confusion never entered. Instead, I swooned to the spell of logic, the orderly lockstep of sentences. How much horror could there be amid such deliberation? And what sorts of turpitude were routinely countenanced in the desire to report, to simply record the events with as bare emotion as possible? What price was paid for this civil calm? How would I know? The trees didn't talk about human endeavors. They were lofty.

Most people in my part of the world were indifferent to the unflappable authority of the *New York Times*. Local events leavened with comics and horoscopes sufficed. I dove most days into the printed pool of human misapprehension, conviction, and wrongdoing without a second thought. It was the fallen world, my *juste milieu*. I had left the urban world to sit by kerosene light in the middle of the woods, where I was as likely to hear a barred owl's unnerving *hoo hoo hoo* as any other sound. What news was in that hooting? It seemed to come from the ancient chest of time itself. Why did I need the endless, fabricated story that the paper supplied me? What didn't I know already? Nothing—that was the point. I remained one of the modern, disaffiliated, ever-curious tribe. The world was so huge, and the headlines that accompanied the stories were understandably redundant—"Human Beings Act As Though They Know What They Are Doing. What Choice Do They Have?"

I walked onto the back porch, my mind full of Serbia, nuclear throw weights, or the demagogue of the hour. Out of doors, it was still and quiet and fresh. No men with Kalashnikovs were marauding. Flares and mortars did not light up the night. I heard no human screams. I was lucky. Geography gave me the space to ponder human intrusiveness—an enlivening yet sobering paradox. Out of doors, I dreamt myself back to a time when people were barely present on the earth. Meanwhile, the unruffled columns testified to our fraught success.

※

The Road Washes Out in Spring

Our daughter was born in a small local hospital. It was a friendly experience, but we wanted our second child to be born where we lived. Birth was a natural event; we wanted that birth to occur in our marriage bed in our house. Our days in the woods were dedicated to the proposition that life was a natural affair. That seemed an unremarkable assertion, but the wiles of human improvement were tireless. Fortified food was better than fresh food. Petroleum-based fertilizer was better than cow shit. Faster travel was better than slower travel. Synthetic fabrics that required less care were better than cotton ones. The list of desirable conveniences extended in every direction. Perpetual amelioration was alluring but tiring; most of it seemed superfluous.

We were naturalists who did not believe that we should live for what science told us. "From my mother's sleep I fell into the State," Randall Jarrell wrote in "The Death of the Ball Turret Gunner." We were skeptical of that corporate, all-knowing State as it offered its manias as facts. We were skeptical of the drone of advertised opinion about what was safe, what was necessary, and what was true. Again and again during the Vietnam War we had been lied to. We resented those lies; we were appalled by those lies and did not forget them. We sought to think our lives through for ourselves on our own forthright terms. We believed that was what freedom was about—the right to be original and enact our feelings on a stage of our own devising. Anyone could believe what he or she was told to believe; anyone could assent to an imperative rant or march to an anthem. Our saying "no" to the automatism of improvement affirmed our backward humanity. It was a "yes" to the chancy joy of living on the earth.

Our doctor agreed with us. He had moved to Maine from Pittsburgh and wanted to practice medicine on his terms, which meant he valued the human exchanges that were part of healing people. He didn't want to see his patients as units he treated at the behest of insurance companies and hospitals whose dictates were driven by money. How could care of the human body be driven by money? He shook his head at some of his fellow doctors who made no bones about refusing to do anything that would put them in jeopardy.

Didn't Craig (our doctor's name) know that the modern world was about exorcising jeopardy? That's why there were insurance policies, protocols, laws, and machines. No one had to stick his or her head out an inch, for part of the fall into the State was the dream of absolute security, of a life not menaced by anything unwanted, where suffering was pushed to the furthest margins of consciousness. The State pursued National Security and did what it pleased on those fearful yet puissant grounds. To invoke the phrase was a reason in its own right. Like The Economy, Security was a capitalized idol that had replaced the haphazard likes of God. As was the case with idols, it was hard to reckon how many lives had been sacrificed in its beneficial name.

Craig knew what he was getting into by doing a home birth; he was calm and happy with it. He had been Janet's physician for years and had delivered our daughter. He knew she had taken care of herself while carrying our child. Although he came prepared, he didn't come overburdened. Indeed, he had room for his wife and two young sons who wanted to experience a home birth firsthand. Craig saw birth as a celebration of what the female body knew and had known for thousands of years. He trusted the strength that had brought the human race this far. He wasn't rash; he was alert. The notion of birth as a sequestered, drugged event saddened him as it saddened us.

Craig knew how we lived. When I called him from our neighbors' house, he was excited and ready. He had a four-wheel-drive, because there was no telling how our road would hold up. Although it was the eighth of May, it had been a cold spring, and there were challenging chasms and soft spots in the road. We had resolutely walked in and out since the road had begun to thaw because we wanted to save on the wear and tear a vehicle would inflict. Since Janet was pregnant, that meant a lot of resolution on her part. She was not deterred. On the contrary, she was buoyant. The walking was part of her bearing a child. Her face glowed with physicality.

I stood by the mailbox outside Stanton and Ella's place holding a flashlight and waiting for Craig and his family to show up. It felt like a very long time. I was way too revved up to stay inside and make halting conversation with Stanton and Ella. We had only been living in the woods since September, but already it felt as if nothing we did would have surprised them. We were the Back-to-the-Land hippies that the newspapers and magazines had been writing about. Now we were having a home birth. There had not been such an occasion in our town for decades. Next we might announce that we were flying to Oregon in a helium balloon or raising iguanas or building a chimney out of bottle caps. We seemed to have no clear sense about what was practical and what was impractical.

I picked up one leg and flexed it at the knee, and then the other leg, a nervous habit. I turned the flashlight off to conserve the batteries and breathed in the cool, moist spring night. Janet's brother, Dave, was up at the house with her, along with our daughter who was almost two. I thought about how odd this all was and how it made deep sense to me. I was the man with the lantern in the darkness who was showing the way. The absence in the country of road signs made it all the more adventuresome. We lived on the first right after you took a right off the state highway. Craig hadn't done anything like a trial run. That would have been the sort of nervous forethought (prudence to some) that none of us indulged in. Everything happened the way it was supposed to happen. "Rain don't fall up," as Caleb in his Zen Maine vein liked to put it.

Craig appeared in what must have been an hour, and I pointed the way. He navigated the dark road quite expertly. Dizzy with adrenaline, I jogged behind him, hollered encouragement, and kept waving the flashlight, though its light was unnecessary. When I saw him pull into the driveway, I was relieved and exhilarated. He had made it to our house. The fact of having traversed our dubious road was an achievement. We would go from there.

And we did. We all introduced ourselves, beginning with, "Hi, I'm Janet. I'm going to have a baby." I made tea and offered cookies. We chatted about the house, the road, what a cold spring it had been, and, of course, babies. We chatted about bringing in wood, growing food, and driving the frost-heaved, pot-holed roads. Susan, Craig's wife, talked about having her children. Her two small sons smiled shyly. Craig examined Janet and said that she was "not yet but almost." Eventually the boys and Susan and Craig bedded down on sofas and chairs. I lay with Janet on our bed. Maisie, our daughter, had gone to sleep a while ago. Dave was up; we listened to the radio—rock and roll. Sometimes we sang along.

Around three Janet started to go into serious labor; our son was born before four o'clock. He came out with the umbilical cord around his neck. I recall Craig ever so deftly severing the cord and Owen, our son, crying lustily. Janet exclaimed, "It's a baby!" Everyone applauded, cheered, and whooped. Our mongrel dog, Webster, barked excitedly. Craig's sons stood wide-eyed. Quickly Janet took Owen to her breast and began to soothe him, then to nurse him. I brought down our daughter to look at her new brother. In the background the radio kept playing; the Byrds were soaring through Bob Dylan's poetic "Mr. Tambourine Man"—another anthem from that tumultuous, idealistic era of hopes, visions, and assassinations. Here was another person in the world. English major that I was, I thought of Lear's "When we are born we cry that we are come / To this great stage of fools."

And here was another sunrise. Craig and his family had driven back down the road. Janet and Owen both were sleeping. I walked with Maisie to the brook near our house. We knelt by the swift, shallow water. I pointed out some trillium on the other side. They were the red ones—not languorously beautiful but vivid and sturdy flowers with their three large petals—and one sign that the northern spring had begun. I was tired and deeply happy. Owen's birth in our own house without the intermediaries of paper forms and fluorescent lights and tall, cold beds mattered. The world he came into was our world. He had come in harmony.

As much as I knew anything I knew that the essence of being human resided in our feelings and that those feelings were as evanescent as the bubbles that my daughter and I were regarding. Their fragility made no difference. They formed the cautionary backdrop and assailable foreground of "the great stage of fools." I could accept that. One intuition that had brought us to the country was that everything is—however slowly or abruptly—moving and becoming. Maisie squealed with delight at the sunlight on the rushing water. "Look!" she shouted in her rapt child's voice. Everything was there.

※

When, in my reading (and I read poetry almost every day), I encountered a poem that I liked, I wrote it down in one of those thick, lined, marbled notebooks with a ruled margin that I had used in grade school. Although a simple act that poets have been doing forever, for me it was a remarkable and valuable chance to recreate in my own hand a creation, to offer homage, experience empathy, indulge curiosity, and hone joy. As I sat there writing at the kitchen table that I had fashioned from an ash tree (our only table), I felt how each word emerged, how each word followed. I felt the certainty of the chosen words and the uncertainty that resided in the pulse of the endeavor, the tremble of spirit. When I wrote a poem down, I was at the patient center of poetry's quicksilver enterprise. I was entering the vulnerable lives of words. I literally was making the poem grow from nothing into its achieved form. Time was reversed, for I was participating in what previously had occurred. I wasn't critiquing, theorizing, expatiating, analyzing, or politicking. I wasn't using the poem as a road to elsewhere. Silently, I was immersing myself in the medium, the mute, entrancing, word by word actuality. That seemed, for the purposes of engaging poetry, sufficient.

Over the years, I found myself romancing some of the most famous poems in the English language. I was at once excited and shy in their presence. I had heard of them, but I was, despite my commitment to poetry, an idiosyncratic reader. Though at times I read steadily through a poet's corpus, I was just as likely to put the book down and pick it up weeks or months later. I might start reading two-thirds of the way through. I might obsessively read the same poem over and over. I might start with a poet's last poems and work backward. Everything depended on my moods. Inspiration was happenstance. I had a horror of "studying" poetry as though it was a subject like geometry or chemistry. Poetry was an environment, a realm, a category of existence, a perennial yet wayward art, a blend of the substantial and the insubstantial, a species of praise. How could one "study" such a fancy? It was an art: it could be spoken about authentically and deftly, but it couldn't be shoehorned into a concept or mastered as a topic. It rebuked systems and implicitly mocked theories. Quietly infinite, it had no use for the limitations of tests. It remained the product of individuals who reveled in their individuality, a pebble dropped into the pond of eternity.

There's a current in poetry that is electric—not metaphorical electricity but a real, static charge, the hoodoo of rhythmic words. I sense that it's going to happen to me—the charge—and anticipate it and want it yet dread it, for it will change me. One never knows how the change will play out. I remember very well sitting down one night after everyone had gone to bed and reading John Keats's "When I Have Fears." I found the poem close to unbearable:

> When I have fears that I may cease to be
>   Before my pen has glean'd my teeming brain,
> Before high-piled books, in charact'ry,
>   Hold like rich garners the full-ripen'd grain;
> When I behold, upon the night's starr'd face,
>   Huge cloudy symbols of a high romance,
> And think that I may never live to trace
>   Their shadows, with the magic hand of chance;
> And when I feel, fair creature of an hour!
>   That I shall never look upon thee more,
> Never have relish in the faery power
>   Of unreflecting love!—then on the shore
> Of the wide world I stand alone, and think
> Till Love and Fame to nothingness do sink.

It seemed a remarkable gift to be able to copy down such a poem. I took my time, because I didn't want the experience to end. I could, of course, memorize the poem, but that wasn't the same thing. Memory made the poem a part of me. What I sought was not so much possession as the teeming thrill of the encounter. I wanted to meet the poem on its own ground. I wanted to write out those exclamation marks myself. I wanted to write out the em dash before "then on the shore" and experience the pause and decision that lie in a mere mark of punctuation. I wanted to feel the richness of Keats's descriptions, his willingness to write a line that has more adjectives in it than nouns—"Huge cloudy symbols of a high romance." I wanted to feel the ticking pulse of the meter. And I wanted to feel, however hard it was, the renunciatory calm of the last lines and the terrible strength of the simple verb, "do sink." In writing the poem down I felt like a pianist who comes to the final, perishing, indomitable note and must let go but doesn't want to.

I preach this writing down of poems to anyone who will listen, particularly those in schools. At first, people are incredulous. "That's awfully old-fashioned, isn't it?" "It takes more time, doesn't it?" "Don't the children find it boring?" When they actually do it, however, something unusual happens. The students start listening; language starts to assume a presence that it didn't have in their lives. The words and lines begin to live as words and lines because the students are experiencing them word by word and line by line. Students start asking questions as to why a word is at the end of a line or why a comma is there. They begin to feel how much cunning and inspiration can go into not many lines. They begin to feel the lives of words.

Poetry believes in the validity of articulate feeling; students come to realize that this society doesn't trust that belief. They hear rumors of poetry's existence in textbooks. They are given occasional, segregated units of poetry to study as a sort of vacation to a foreign land. The clear implication is that poetry is not something to live with and make part of one's life. It isn't practical. It resists reduction and redaction; it is intellectually fluky. It revels in emotion and human subjectivity. It prefers the tangles of mystery and intimation; it is—in a word—trouble. In schools, poetry breeds anxiety, for typically it is accompanied by the horrendous question, "Now what does the poem mean?"

It's sad because all poetry asks is to be given a chance—to be heard and be taken respectfully. It's the respect that is problematic, because respect implies attentiveness and caring. A society obsessed with pragmatic purposefulness focuses on words as approximate communicators. Words are myrmidons; they live to bear the burdens of situational meaning. That they have a life of their own is beside the point; that any given word is a source of energy, beauty, fanciful utility, and history is unnerving.

In prosperous America, it is the legacy of Puritan absolutism and insecurity that rejects the pleasurable individuality of poetry, that goes in fear of the untrammeled word. As Emily Dickinson testified, the Puritan mind wants to subdue the word the way it wants to subdue the world (a mere letter more), according to the Omnipotence who assuages his followers with the blandishments of salvation. Poetry lives its numinous life outside of Scripture; it smacks of the pagan world and offers an unallowable, counter life. Even when subdued, as genteel Christianity has tried hard to do, to the dictates of sententious abstractions and Nature-as-spiritual-vapor, poems are still untrustworthy. Like memories, they can be cherished and pondered for something like forever. They have that arresting, exhilarating aroma of the sheer incredibility of existence.

The Puritan intuition is unapologetic (as Dickinson well knew), for it senses that the emotional smolder of poetry comprises a challenge to the Puritan God's all-disposing power; even a small feeling is a world unto itself. Poetry recognizes that little is laid out for us as human beings beyond our mortality. When I try to imagine a changed world, I imagine people taking the time to write down the likes of John Keats. When I am in a classroom dictating some lines to students, it is a revelation—though one with an un-capitalized r.

※

The richness of the earth, the fact that a properly nurtured seed will grow into a plant, can produce a giddiness in those who grew up with cement and asphalt instead of soil. Who dreamt while strolling through the dazed and distracted aisles of a warehouse-like grocery store that the earth was connected to this abundance? Since most of what one sees are boxes, cans, jars, bottles, and the enticements written thereon, the focus on what is edible fades into what is packageable. In a vast, fluorescent, cinderblock grocery store, the earth, as the producer of food, seems very distant. The origins of the fruits and vegetables—to say nothing of the meat—are not discussed. They exist as if divorced from any terrestrial location. Capitalism and its handmaid science summoned them up.

The deception, hucksterism, and dislocation that shrouded food were opposed by the heady myth of "living off the land" (or "living on the land"—despite the opposite prepositions, the two phrases hailed from the same mindset). When we first moved to Maine, bought acreage, and started meeting others who were pursuing a similar path, the notion came up regularly, as in, "I'm thinking of growing my own food and living off the land." Though hindsight might dismiss such notions as delusions (as hindsight is prone to do), it seems unfair to write off the feelings behind them. Those feelings stem from an understandable desire to be accountable for one's being in basic ways. The food we take into our mouths is of great matter to us. "Grow your own" often referred to the culture of marijuana, but it also referred to growing vegetables, legumes, fruits, and grains. The attitude was clear: if you can't take the time to grow some of what you eat, what are you doing here on earth? That food should be the province of corporations concerned with their profit margins was a harsh commentary on the confused efficiencies of mass societies. Convenience thwarted authenticity, because authenticity involved some work, some nurture, and some perseverance. Convenience enabled people to forget about the earth. Better to heed an ad than grub in the dirt.

Nothing pleased us better than grubbing in that dirt—right down to the earthworms going about their slimy, crucial work. Robert Frost had counseled his readers to "build soil"; we took him seriously. As the basis of how we lived, soil was the first culture. A healthy society had healthy soil. When we tossed potato peels, squash skins, and bean pods into the compost pile, we felt an earnest pleasure. We weren't indifferent. We cared about making our tiny bit of earth prosper. We were here not just to use what was at hand but to make it as vital as we could make it.

We hauled cow shit, chicken shit, horse shit, and probably some kinds of shit I have forgotten. We dug and hoed and forked—no gas-powered Rototiller for us. We watered—can by patient can.

We fenced to keep out the deer, moose, woodchucks, and hares that wanted to have their share of our produce. We carefully stored our potatoes, cabbages, and carrots in bins and barrels in the root cellar. There, deep in the earth, they would keep through the long winter. The root cellar was the foundation for the children's bedrooms, which we had added on to the original house. It had high cement walls; the floor was pea stone laid over bare earth. We accessed this dark, fragrant kingdom via a trap door and set of wooden stairs. I loved pulling aside the newspapers that covered the potatoes, reaching around and feeling their various textures, then pulling some out and covering them up again. They sat in a tall bin I had built of studs and scrap plywood, another funky design that came from the order of our lives.

Our vegetable garden was extensive—the equivalent of ten twenty-foot rows that were four-feet wide. Though we never "lived off the land," we grew a goodly amount of our own food. We processed and stored it, too, our chief ritual being the canning of tomatoes at summer's end. That meant tending around two dozen tomato plants. Though tomatoes grow like weeds, we had to prop them up, keep a more or less daily eye out for pests and blights, side-dress them with nutrients, lop off unwanted limbs, and cover them when the frosts began. Then there was the canning process, which meant taking the skins off after immersing them briefly in hot water, coring them, cutting them up, putting them in canning jars, placing the lids on those jars, screwing on the rings that held the lids in place, placing the jars in the big, water-filled canner that we had heated up on our little gas stove, and gently boiling that canner for the better part of an hour. Then we would carefully take out the jars, let them cool, clean them, place them on shelves in the root cellar, and clean the canner and rings for their next use. This took many hours and was done by Janet and me over a series of September days. We put up thirty to forty quarts. Once upon a time, there were summer kitchens where women did this hot work. We kept the screen doors and windows open and sweated freely.

Was this economical? The seeds from which we grew the tomato seedlings cost something. The tools with which we gardened cost something. The fence cost something. The nutrients we used in addition to our own compost cost something. The canning jars cost something. The propane we used cost something. And on and on. I'm sure it could be shown that we were losing money by canning our own food. It was one more soft-headed romance. The question we asked in return was, "Is it economical to be a human being?" Probably not.

Our canned tomatoes constituted one basis for our winter menus —chili, minestrone, and pasta sauce being three mainstays. Going down into the root cellar and fetching a jar off the shelves was a contented moment. These were our tomatoes; we were taking them into our bodies. We noted how some jars had more liquid than others, how some tomatoes had yellow streaks where they hadn't quite ripened. We noted the different tastes of different tomatoes— some richer, some thinner, some more acidic. Like us, they weren't uniform.

We knew a few people who literally did live off the land. They grew everything they used, literally pressing their own cooking oil from sunflower seeds they grew, making bread that was ground from their own wheat berries, and plowing with a draft horse for whom they raised oats that they threshed themselves. They worked harder than anyone I knew yet did it gladly. Zealots for self-reliance, their eyes gleamed with a worn intensity. In their carefully patched overalls, straw hats, and worn bandanas, they were living the perennial life. What the commercial world called "drudgery" was their joy.

Their labor was an old American dream. Jefferson had dreamt about it when he conceived of a nation of small farmers who took care of themselves and who could grow and barter most of their sustenance. There was no ulterior dynamic to this existence, no excitement in the sense of marketing and advertising. It was buried in the great wheel of the seasons, the dogged efforts humans must make, and the tribulations—drought, insects, storms—humans must face. It accepted the earth as the first and foremost reality. It believed that virtue and satisfaction resided in steady contact with the soil. It believed in roots—real ones that sank deep. It believed that a thriving orchard or a field of buckwheat or timothy was as inspiring a sight as a person would ever lay eyes on.

This was easy enough for a slave-owning, traveling-abroad, wine-imbibing gentleman farmer to propose. Though our neighbors looked back with nostalgia at the world of small farms that had existed not that long ago in our county, they didn't regret the labors they had given up. If anything, they felt as though they had been gulled. City people were pushing papers around, while they were rising at four in the morning to do chores to make not much money, to live in a world that always wanted more money. No wonder their children had moved away and the quick-to-sprout aspen and pine had reclaimed so many farms. They wished us well in our little, amateur endeavors. They smiled indulgently when we showed them a prize pumpkin or made a gift of a head of lettuce. In the vast scheme of manufacturing and mega-farming, our homespun economy wasn't even a pinpoint. That didn't bother us. As newcomers to the land, no lure ran deeper nor meant more. We may have lived on a dead-end, dirt road in the middle of so-called nowhere, but we weren't exiled from the earth.

Urban people frequently told us that our lives were an "idyll." There we were in the Maine woods with no sirens screaming, homeless people importuning, subways lurching, or auto security systems wailing. We were living what the gurus of the Back-to-the-Land Movement, Helen and Scott Nearing, once forthrightly (if smugly) called "the good life." The chickadees darted to the feeder. The deer browsed under the ancient apple trees. The seasons followed one another in a simple yet intricate dance. We predicted the weather from the sky and the wind. All was as it should be.

When a coyote leaped at an emaciated deer's throat, when an owl dove and seized an unwary mouse, or when a fisher eviscerated a beloved house cat (Ella lost cats routinely), this idyllic aspect blurred. We tend to observe nature on a picturesque day rather than a typical one. On a typical one, if one's eyes and ears are open, the great equation of living and dying is inevitably being played out. Sitting as we do at the top of the food chain, we are not inclined to look down from our eminence. Our understandable inclination is not to keep our eyes and ears unnecessarily open, to take what we want and leave the bloody rest.

The rest includes the human beings who live their lives on the hither and yon roads that the postal service designates as Rural Free Delivery. What we witnessed in our small town (and what I knew of in the somewhat larger town where I worked) were sporadic, violent explosions that resulted in murder. These were, to a degree, categorical: men who had lost their women and whose revenge on those women was to kill them. Or women who were abused by their men and reached a breaking point. One winter night one of my former students came home drunk as usual after hanging out with his buddies and downing beer after beer after beer. He commenced slapping his girlfriend around. She ran into another room, came back with a handgun, and shot him three times. He died there in the kitchen of their trailer. I remembered him as blond, not averse to raising hell, and hailing from a family of like-minded brothers, one of whom had done time in the state prison. He had an impish, little boy smile. He never seemed mean to me, but I wasn't around him when he was ugly-drunk.

I doubt if Bobby (his name) ever took a walk in the woods for the sake of taking a walk. I doubt if he ever stood in those woods and listened for the sake of listening. That wasn't part of his life. That was something out-of-state people did who were admirers of nature and tended to be gentle, squeamish souls who watched birds. Bobby, as I recall, liked to ride snowmobiles, four-wheelers, and dirt bikes. Anything with an engine was good with him—the louder the better. The woods all around him were a playground of old logging roads and trails that he could zoom around on. "I like the throttle open and the muffler busted," as one of my students once put it. The bumpier the path, the better.

Though it may seem unbelievable, three different murders were perpetrated within a radius of a few miles from us. From where we lived you could walk the mile or two to Randall and Marsha's tiny

Cape. An older couple, they had lived their entire lives in our town and worked in a shoe factory. Marsha's brother, Frank, lived across the road and lunched with them every day—biscuits, meat, canned vegetables, layer cake for dessert with strong coffee. Frank worked on his own in the woods and was famous for having survived a tree falling on him. Although he had a broken leg (to say nothing of shock) and was pinned beneath the tree, he dug himself out, crawled to his truck, got in, and drove to the hospital. I heard the story from others, because Frank barely talked to anyone. I did notice his limp. He lived by himself in a farmhouse that had seen better days. His wife had left long ago. The word in town was that he drank, but so did a lot of people. It seemed that everyone either drank a lot or didn't drink at all. The middle ground was hard to find.

Randall and Marsha let it be known that they were planning to move to South Carolina to live near their daughter who was married with children. The winters were starting to get too hard for them, Randall told me. He was a great cribbage player, Bible reader, and Red Sox fan. Now that he was retired (without any pension to show for his decades of work), he had a modest woodworking shop where he turned out medicine cabinets, side tables, and birdhouses from pine boards. He made us a stand to hold an unabridged *Webster's Dictionary* that we still have. I used to hang out with him while he puttered around the shop. In summer we listened on the radio to the Red Sox. He was one of those Red Sox fans who combined love of the game with sturdy pessimism about his team. Every time we listened, Randall told me about seeing Ted Williams play: "Did I ever tell you I saw the great Ted Williams play?" "No," I lied. "Well let me tell you, Mister Man. No one ever swung a bat as smooth as Ted Williams."

Year-round Marsha cooked for the three of them. They ate at one of those small, dinette tables that had been popular in the fifties. One day when Frank came over for their regular mid-day meal, he brought his rifle with him. Who can imagine what Randall and Marsha thought when they saw that rifle, they who had eaten with him thousands of times and made small talk about the weather and the state of the road that ran between their opposing houses? He shot Randall and Marsha dead and then killed himself. They weren't going to South Carolina and leave him alone.

I knew the woman who found the bodies. She stopped by to deliver a pint of strawberry jelly to Marsha, have a cup of tea, and chat. Nothing ever happened on that road. A few cars went by each hour. The school bus went up and down the road around six thirty in the morning and then again around three thirty. At Marsha and Randall's, squirrels tried to get at the suet hung on a cedar pole, and blue jays squawked at the feeder. That was about it. When she walked in and saw the blood on the walls and the bodies, she began screaming. She was a levelheaded woman, but she said that all she could do was scream until she collapsed. What she saw was something that didn't happen in a small town. Randall and Marsha were the mildest, dearest people. Who, in his or her right mind, would ever expect such bloodshed? But then again, who in the back of his or her not right mind, didn't? Small town didn't mean peaceful town.

Dark feeling doesn't evaporate. It lingers and rankles. It eats us from the inside, a slow process that the bottle encourages. We do unto ourselves before we do unto others. Sometimes, however, the darkness blows. When an enraged, drunken man in his thirties shot through a front door to show his two-timing female companion that he meant business and, with that bullet, killed a boy who was in the house, I can't say I saw it coming, but I can't say I was surprised. Or when the husband of the town clerk came into the town office and shot her right there, the woman who was divorcing him and in love with another man, I was even less surprised. He was a quiet guy who seemed wound too tight. After killing her, he went home, set fire to their farmhouse, and turned the gun on himself. By the time the volunteer fire department got there, the place was largely gone. When, that day, I saw smoke spiraling in the sky to the north of our place—black, roiling gobs—I thought of war.

That one happened in late spring. Poppies were starting to bloom, warblers were everywhere, and you could smell the pale, divine scent of lilacs that stood in front of the old homesteads. She was buried on a beautiful day. People tried to say consoling things while staring ahead dully. It was idyllic in that country graveyard, but the irony of the statement comes too easily. As humans we are open to the world around us and instinctively feel ties that bind us to the hills and rivers and clouds. Where those feelings go is hard to say beyond the fact of their fading into the daily melee, yet we have the chance to find something within us beyond will. Perhaps, because few of us intimately depend on the natural world, that relationship seems tangential, at best. And when the confusions of jealousy and hurt rear their heads, the deep equanimity of earth and sky doesn't matter. No one can count the ways that love can go wrong. The flower has nothing to say to the man with a gun and a bad look in his eyes. Perhaps he never saw that flower in the first place. That's who many men are.

I smelled the lilacs beside the village church and breathed the fragrance in deeply. In the scheme of American striving, taking the time to appreciate anything or anyone seems beside the point. A professor once told a class I was in that we weren't there to appreciate poems—we were there to analyze them. His voice made me feel as though we were going to whip some raw recruits into shape. But wasn't appreciation the cardinal aspect of our being alive? And didn't it need nurturing? And wasn't the soft, delicious drift of that lilac scent vital as it spoke to all that we could never create or control but that accompanied us in this world? That was some of what I wanted to say to my fellow mourners as we walked back to our cars to resume our hopeful lives. Tourists driving by on the state highway might have commented on the funeral in the old, picturesque cemetery and on the country folk in their stiff, best clothes. It was hard not to be a tourist.

※

Though Mac ran the local store and forthrightly called it "Mac's," it was common to think of the store as the town's store. It was the place where people met and made community small talk about which roads were in the worst shape, who was putting a new roof on their house, how at dusk six deer had been sighted at the crest of

Cedar Hill. When a person walked into the store in the morning, there was an official greeter of sorts—Frank Hale—who stood by the front door leaning on his cane and saying "good morning" to whomever came in. Frank, who was in his eighties, lived by himself. Everyone knew Frank was still alive because he came into the store each day. "Reporting in," Frank called it in his kind, wobbly, old man's voice. When someone in town had died and Mac put a sympathy card out for people to sign, Frank would point to the card and crow, "Not yet. No card for me yet." He smiled with the most genuine delight—glad to be alive another day. Mac treated him to a coffee each morning.

The building was a humble, shed-roof structure Mac put up in the early 1970s. It wasn't an old-time general store from the nineteenth century with a wooden porch out front, high, pressed-tin ceilings, worn, wide floorboards, long counters, glass cabinets, and a painted sign hanging out front. You had to go to the next town for one of those. Mac's cement-floor store was crammed with the basics—automotive oil, two-cycle oil, bar and chain oil, beer, candy, milk, chips, hot dogs, cookies, potatoes, and, after the state liquor agency loosened up and let stores carry hard liquor, coffee brandy and whiskey. No olive oil, garlic, spice rack, or bottle of imported wine took up valuable space. There was a counter off to the side where you could get a "real Mac"—a hefty hamburger with fried onions and green peppers. Truckers and other connoisseurs of the grill made a point of stopping at Mac's for a filling, greasy meal. "Nutrition be damned" might have been Mac's slogan. A sign lettered on the storefront read, "Eat Here, Get Gas." Mac himself was a world-class burper.

Mac's was open from six in the morning until eight at night. He could have opened at five, and he could have closed at nine or ten, but he wanted a few hours in the day to call his own. The store was open seven days a week. He and his wife worked in the store, as did his children when they got into their early teens, though that, of course, was temporary. "Too bad you can't keep them one age for more than one year," Mac used to say. He had help, too—local women who figured the convenience of working nearby was worth the modest pay. Plus they got to know everything that was going on in town. Gossip wasn't money, but it made life interesting.

Dealing with the public was never easy. People left the faucets on in the restroom or crapped on the restroom floor ("Happens a couple of times each summer," Mac told me), shoplifted, complained about prices ("This isn't what the grocery store in Skowhegan charges"), tried to wheedle information that wasn't their business, or didn't pay their bills (Mac let townspeople run tabs for groceries). Mac's way of dealing with the miscellaneous human race was to act as though the store was a stage and the customers theatergoers. He emoted, orated, complained, philosophized, lamented, and—best of all— sang. I mean really cut-loose, belt-it-out, shake-the-rafters sing. He was in a barbershop quartet that went to national competitions, and he walked around the store delivering in his strong tenor one Amer- ican classic after another. No one quite knew what to make of this lyrical behavior, but people seemed happy enough to hear "Casey Jones" or "The Streets of Laredo." Unless you went to a tavern to hear wretched covers of British hair bands or mainstream Nashville or you went to church on Sunday morning, you didn't hear anyone singing in public. Mac took care of that.

On any given day, Mac was engaged in a conversation with him- self that he allowed his customers to eavesdrop on or interrupt if they had the temerity. He referred to himself in the third person, as in, "Mac, if you don't order more donuts, people are going to get very upset." Or, "Mac, haven't you nibbled enough peanut brittle for the day?" It was hard to resist snacking on your own merchan- dise; Mac wasn't one to turn down the bevy of modest temptations spread before him. His girth was part of his cheer; "confection" was one of his favorite words. He once instructed me never to trust a thin storekeeper.

It doesn't get much more democratic than a small town. Everyone who has lived there a while matters in some particular way, every- one has a place in the town's lore, everyone is entitled to be whoever he or she is. Personality—the bumptious sense of what someone is like—still thrived. You could say a person was stubborn, hot- tempered, or flighty and not append a story about the woes that had caused such behavior. The notion of people as victims hadn't penetrated our corner of the world, where bumper stickers announced, "God, Guns and Guts Made This Country Great." The contemporary, beckoning totem of Change wasn't very powerful in rural Maine. People were what they were and were proud of it.

It was Mac's task to get along with all opinions and behaviors. He did this by cultivating the cash nexus: "I'm happy to meet your money," was a standard greeting. He did this by making gentle (and occasionally not so gentle) fun of everyone. "You still driving that beater? The market is good for scrap metal, you know," was a standard gibe. He did this by agreeing with everyone, "I'm not a Democrat or a Republican. I'm a storekeeper." He did this by greeting any assertion with the words, "Is that right?" He did this by preserving a sliver of inner space, by not being there even when he was right in front of you. "Where was I?" was a question he asked many times each day. Despite his waistline, he floated through the store's stuffy, dust-laden, faintly rancid air.

With his endless singing he parodied cheerfulness, yet he had the good nature to face each fourteen-hour day and the various slices of humanity our town represented. He shook his head at what people did to him and to others but refused to lose faith in them. He was intimate with people—he knew their lives inside out—but remained respectful. He was not one to pry. And there was no doubt that he reveled in being a proprietor. He wasn't working shifts for a corporation in Boston. He owned the store. After a Little League win, he would treat the team to ice cream. The kids would sit out in front of the store while Mac saluted each player for his or her effort. It looked like quintessential small town America—bicycles and mitts everywhere, the kids in their baggy uniforms, and someone's mutt hanging around looking for a handout—and it was. Whatever other trouble there was in town, there were clear moments of communal generosity—people putting up stove wood for someone who was hurt, or people organizing a dinner to raise money for someone who was sick and uninsured. When he moved his family to North Carolina and an office job ("I'm tired," he confessed one day to me), he sold to an anxious little man who chain-smoked, joked nervously, and smiled painfully. He was thin, and the store—despite the good-will Mac had created—began a downward slide. Without Mac's vo-calizing, it was dreary. It could have been anywhere.

✼

The dominant season in the north is winter. Summer is a tease, a passing delight, a distraction, an intense but brief affair. In July the heat obviates the memory of the cold. In the early morning we are free to lie in bed and drowse, a flimsy cotton blanket covering us. We don't scurry downstairs from our sleeping loft to light a fire in the cook stove, the way we do most of the year. We aren't schlep-ping wood in a couple times a day; the wood boxes (there are two in the house) are abandoned to the spiders. We don't think about the frosts that are going to blacken the basil and curl the zucchini leaves. The spring frosts—don't plant your tomatoes until Memorial Day—are history, and the autumn frosts—full moon in Septem-ber—aren't there yet. We dream of the earth's heat, and we feel the earth's heat. It is a romance.

People who live in the north pride themselves on winter's fierce-ness. The cold's fortitude presents a direct challenge to human for-titude. We relished it and loved hearing stories from Stanton, Ella, and Caleb about winters in the old days when people got around on snowshoes, sleighs, and sleds. Stanton had a pair of proto-cross-country skis in his barn that he claimed were made of hickory. They were light, long, and thin and lacquered heavily to resist the water. He assured us that he used to get around on them "real slick."

Mere surviving doesn't seem a high aim, yet the Maine winter makes a person respect how daunting those months can be. Since we heated totally with wood, winter took our attention throughout the year. The endless handling of wood—log by log and stick by stick—made the rigors of snowstorms and below-zero cold snaps al-most sweet. The woodpile dwindled, but we remained comfortably ahead, knowing from experience that four to five cords of wood would see us through a winter. Just in case, we had an extra cord on hand. Already I was felling trees for next winter. As I clomped around on a January day, I was living in the moment—my fingers as they tried to grip the chainsaw felt more rigid than supple—but I was also living in the future of another winter, a further hill that I knew was there.

Life seemed endless; those months when the thermometer rarely went over the freezing mark were as close to eternity as we were going to experience. The gray days of spitting snow and the crystalline days of cold sun and arctic blue sky seemed to keep time at bay; winter was weighty and in no hurry. Yet eternity did pass; stern winter ran from mid-December to mid-February. However slowly, the sun was climbing higher in the sky; the days were getting longer. The solace of the light was profound. When we observed the late January light that lingered at five o'clock, it was a calm, almost amazed feeling. No matter that the temperature read zero. The promising light was there.

There was plenty of misery to winter. Cars didn't start (no engine warmer for us or even a garage, for that matter), and I found myself pushing the Subaru down the hill in front of our house while Janet turned the key and pumped the gas in hopes of the engine turning over. Some mornings that worked; other mornings it didn't. We climbed on the roof to bang off ice dams on the north side of the house with the back of a hatchet or a hammer. I cleaned the outside chimney periodically with a feedbag that I had stuffed with straw and bricks. Very carefully, I moved around on the peak of the roof that often was slick with ice and snow to position myself beside the chimney's top. It wasn't that high—our house was a Cape—but it was high enough. I lowered the bag that was attached to a long, heavy rope and gently swung it to knock off creosote that had built up on the sides of the tiled liner that, if left untended, could clog the chimney or catch on fire. When I cleaned the creosote out of the door at the base of the chimney, it looked like hardened lava. The first time I saw those black sheets I remember thinking that this is the most primitive substance I have ever laid eyes on. Even in the sterile cold, it had a smoky, inky smell. Though I knew it would break down and go back to Mother Earth, the process was hard to imagine. It was like trying to imagine bones or teeth rotting. It was recalcitrant stuff.

Over the course of the winter, our skin turned into the consistency of old leather. When we went for walks, the cold drilled into our foreheads, making us sensitive to cavities we never thought twice about. Even our obdurate skulls were vulnerable. We thought of the deer bedded down beneath the conifers, the red squirrels juking around on the snow crust, and the nuthatches flitting back and forth, back and forth from the pines to the feeder. How did they do it? Their blood was unbelievable. Their metabolisms made the backbeat of rock and roll pale. They were the wild things who rightfully inherited the earth. We, meanwhile, wore layers upon layers of clothes and felt like living mummies. Some nights we cranked the wood stoves so we could lounge around in T-shirts and remember our flesh and sweat.

In the winter we drew inward. By nature, summer was expansive. We gardened, hiked, swam, went on berry-picking expeditions, laid up wood, and did whatever needed to be done on the outside of the house. Winter, however, meant long nights inside. For a writer this seasonal rhythm seemed perfect. I could brood forever while the dark night said nothing. I could sit and listen to the fires sputter and hiss as if they were the silver tongues of fancy. The pale flame of language murmured as we sat by the Jøtul stove and read book after book. Summer echoed the tropical, untutored ease of paradise, but our life on the winter earth felt unnatural—like the letters on the book's page that didn't exist anywhere in nature. Imperfect hibernators that we were, winter taxed us yet released us into the fields of imagination. The ground had literally disappeared beneath the snow; spring was a distant rumor. We read, talked, drank the Bancha tea we favored, and talked more. Banished for a time, we waited, mused, and dreamed.

I could sit with my poems and sift them, turn them on their heads, kick the tires—whatever metaphor I chose to describe the process of reaching my beguiling but unattainable ideal. I liked this activity as much as, maybe more, than the first, imaginative rush of the poem. I could shape something that I had made. It combined contemplation and alacrity, yoking the ping of inspiration to the tireless task of finding the best words. As I sat there with my pencil, I thought of women knitting and men whittling wood in the long nights of prior eras. I thought of people putting down volumes with a sigh. What will Mr. Dickens think of next? I thought of the lethargy of the seemingly endless nights and the yawns of children taking warmed, flat stones to bed with them to keep themselves cozy. I thought of hot milk and cocoa, of cats dozing like time itself. I thought of the human voice reciting poems, Bible passages, tall tales, remembrances. I thought of the silences, too, of regret and reverie and longing, of the taut eloquence of unexpressed reproach and watchful eyes.

Occasionally the night did speak: trees boomed and creaked as their fibers shivered in the cold. A timber in our little house groaned. The woods formed an eerie chorus; even the dimension lumber that held up our walls muttered to itself. They might be human cries; they called to mind Dante's hell and the torments of lost souls. Disconcerted, I listened attentively but heard nothing further. Gradually, the uneasy quiet softened. I was lulled once again. I put another length of maple into the long box stove and closed down the draft to a penny's width.

When in the middle of the night I stepped onto the back porch to piss into a snow bank (a rural, male amenity of sorts), I craned my neck to peek at the pure, unbelievable stars. Awe held me until the cold raised goose bumps. Back inside, I raked the embers in the stove forward, put in more wood, and waited a few, staring, hypnotic seconds for the fire to flare up. My wife sighed in her sleep when I got back into bed. We were cradled in the arms of a heartless nurse. We loved her.

＊

As much as anything that went with our living in the woods, we wanted a hearth—a fire that we could kindle each day and on which to cook our food. Since Janet and I both grew up in modernized households, I'm not sure where the idea came from. I have a feeling that it is a genetic idea, something encoded in our blood. I had never heard of a cast-iron cook stove before I came to Maine.

A stove ran on gas or electricity. There was no making of fires involved. You turned a knob or pushed a button, and there was the
heat to cook your food. Such cooking was relatively neat. Whenever
there was smoke in my childhood kitchen, it meant my mom had
burnt a piece of meat, not that the stovepipe wasn't drawing well.

Before we moved into our house in the woods, we rented a small
farmhouse from a school teacher I knew. She had retired and had
gone with her husband to live in Vermont. She left behind a cook
stove on which was stamped the manufacturer, the city and state in
which it was made—Bangor, Maine—and the year—1924. The
stove was squat and black with ample room on the top for pots
and pans. It had an oven, water tank, firebox, various draft con-
trols to manage the fire, and clean-out pan for the ashes. With a little refurbishing, such as getting the water tank re-soldered so that
it wouldn't leak, we had ourselves a real, cast-iron cook stove. It
weighed what felt like a ton but came apart fairly easily. We paid
fifty dollars for it.

That stove became the hearth of our imaginings. Most mornings of the year we started a fire in it to warm the house and heat
up hot water. On top of the stove stood a canning kettle for that
purpose. We dipped a pan into that kettle for hot water, which we
then poured into a metal wash basin to wash hands and faces. I
shaved each morning in that basin while using a small mirror that I
propped against the rear of the kitchen sink. The water varied from
cool to agreeably lukewarm to hot. For a habitual experience, it was
far from routine. While shaving, I sometimes recalled how various
nineteenth-century eminences (Emerson and Thoreau, for instance)
told of waking on a winter morning and discovering that ice had
formed in the wash water in the bedroom jug. Little wonder that
Yankees tended to be brisk.

The cook stove took small pieces of wood—cut-up tree limbs
were ideal. Some visitors wondered at the stack of long "sticks" that
I kept near the woodsheds and sawed into ten-inch lengths. They
didn't look like wood that a serious woodcutter would bother with.
They were right; a guy cutting pulpwood or logs for a lumber mill
would not have cared less. After a few hours running the chainsaw,

I felt serious enough, however. If there was a category for ethical woodcutters, those devoted to using fully what the earth gave forth, I would have checked that box. As a household we were string savers, wire savers, bag savers. Whereas packaging that existed to be thrown out captivated the society at large, we were saving broom and mop handles to stake our tomatoes with.

We started our fires with old newspapers. That meant a degree of lollygagging some less-than-frigid mornings when Janet or I became involved in a news item and forgot about warming up the house. Eventually, after a comment on the troubled state of the world, the fire would be started with the crumpled newspaper and some kindling I had split. Typically the kindling was from one of the local hardwood mills—cubes and rectangles that were part of the trimmings engendered in producing yo-yos, toy trains, and cabinet handles. Sometimes the kindling was softwood—edgings from hemlock or fir that were tossed aside when the tree was de-barked and made suitable for milling. Whatever the kindling was, I placed each piece on a stout round of maple that sat near the back porch and split it with a hatchet into thin lengths that would catch fire easily. In no time I had a good-sized pile.

Most days we cooked on the wood-fired stove. It was great for frying, for simmering soups, for baking casseroles. We had a small gas stove that we also used because our cooking and fire building weren't always in synch. Usually, though, we were in synch; the cook stove was more than symbolic. In deep winter we kept it going for warmth and made soups that required hours to cook. I became enamored of split pea soup because it took forever. It thickened, and I diluted it. It thickened again, and I diluted it. Or Janet made baked beans. Again, it was an all-day dish as it cooked slowly in the oven. To go along with the beans, she made brown bread and coleslaw with cabbage that we had grown. When we ate such a meal we felt—despite our Jewish surnames—like bona fide New Englanders. The howling wilderness they had feared had been tamed and cultivated and then abandoned. The quilt of fields had returned to woods that had their share of wild creatures. We were celebrating a lost heritage.

Every day we cooked from scratch—soups, casseroles, stir fries, omelets, pasta dishes, sautés, salads. There was neither microwave nor freezer. For something resembling refrigeration, we relied for many years on a box that hung below the house from the kitchen floor and was opened by a small trap door. We used the floor of the root cellar, too. There was no take-out available in town beyond Mac's, whose pizzas didn't tempt us. Our meals were at the center of our lives, which was where we wanted them to be. We weren't too hassled to cook what we had taken the time to grow—asparagus in late spring, new potatoes as soon as they could be dug, berry desserts in late summer, root crops and *brassicas*—carrots, potatoes, cabbage, and beets—in the winter. We grew alfalfa sprouts, which our kids threw out of their school lunches because they looked weird to the other kids. We milled our own flour from hard, red Montana wheat in a little, hand-cranked Corona mill. Janet made bread regularly. Despite its strange brown color, our kids didn't throw out the bread. It was too delicious.

We believed in our food. That sounds strange—why wouldn't people believe in what they took into their bodies—but corporate food and the agri-business (a truly unappealing word) seem unbelievable to me. I understand ease, hygiene, efficient, mammoth machines, advertising, novelty, and not having enough time (America's epitaph will be, "They Were Busy"), but food is a daily, sustaining ritual. If the preparation, presentation, and consumption of food are careless, a sad pattern has been set. It becomes fuel more than food, packaged sustenance for people whose minds are on other things. It exists for harried ghosts. The animals whose lives are being given to them are not realities. Ghosts don't need to know where their food comes from; their substance is convenience.

We gravitated instinctively to peasant economies where food was at the center of life. Grow it, cook it, eat it, share it, and celebrate it. Go to market at places where you have a sense of who grew the food and produced the food. Basic tastes and textures were compasses— the fermented tang of miso, the satisfying mass of oatmeal, the tartness of cranberries, the sweetness of winter squash. The notion of improving on such an economy seemed idle. Had anyone improved on fresh, handmade pasta? Had anyone improved on a red sauce made with your own tomatoes, garlic, and oregano? The home-made applesauce cooked from apples we harvested from wild apple trees, the granola I made batch by batch, the muffins, biscuits, and breads Janet baked were part of our commitment to firsthand food. Cooking was a venerable art; we wanted to honor it. When people told us that they were too busy ever to cook, we inwardly flinched. Sitting down to eat food we had grown and cooked affirmed our taking the time to be in our own lives.

Through the seasons, the cook stove hearth remained. I see myself looking down at a big, black fry pan—what they used to call a "spider" in Maine—and the diced potatoes I was making into hashed browns. I have the fire in the stove right where I want it. The heat is coming out full force, and the stovetop is almost glowing. Those potatoes are going to fry fast and crisp. They are Kennebecs. I like them best for these purposes—firm white flesh that embraces the frying oil, paprika, onions, and salt. Most summers we grow three different kinds of potatoes for different cooking purposes. I feel the heat coming off the stove, and I can smell it—the keen, thick scent of burning hardwood. It is the aboriginal scent of fire and food. I am watching the potatoes and turning them over when they start to brown, and then they are ready. On top of the potatoes we pour spicy, rich ketchup that we have made from our tomatoes and canned. It's not elaborate cooking, but it tastes terrific. The feeling that goes with the cooking is an old one—we are happy when we are making something. When children play, they construct elaborate worlds out of mud, dolls, sticks, and words. The daily chore of making another meal wasn't a chore. Perhaps a degree of amazement never left us—that we could take care of ourselves in such a basic, satisfying way, that our food and the very fire on which we cooked could be our own.

❧

The cooking, woodcutting, and reading were equal elements of an integral life. We wanted books to have the passion and texture of clear-eyed originality. The notion of a book as a holiday from reality or touted "good read" didn't do much for us. We wanted to encounter something that would move and surprise us. When I started to read the Polish poets—especially Czeslaw Milosz, Zbigniew Herbert, Wislawa Szymborska—in translation, I felt, "Ah, this is what I have been waiting for. This is it." "It" meant the depth of history grounded in individual art so scrupulous it could take the measure of the monstrosities of the twentieth century.

As an American, I hadn't thought much about Poland. For someone who grew up in the 1950s, it was one of those countries behind the Iron Curtain; one of history's unfortunates that moldered in the desiccating dust of communism while the West went its electric way. It lacked the élan of revolutionary Latin America; the United States wasn't embroiled in a war there. "What else," my ignorance said, "was there?" I thought occasionally of the hopeless mammoth that was post-Stalinism, of a repression that blew on the dead embers of ideology and proclaimed the genius of its wrongheaded ways. I recalled pictures of the Polish cavalry opposing the Nazi tanks and took this gesture to be quintessential. How could courage survive in a society where inertia seemed the motive force?

What I came to experience through the poets was that Poland was not on the periphery. On the contrary, it was at the center of the century. Precisely because it had been waylaid, abandoned, lied to, traduced, and then pocketed like some weighty if not particularly valuable old coin, it had a front-row seat on several strains of political derangement that passed for dynamism in modern times. Geography is fate, and though it wasn't a seat many people would have chosen, it was a remarkable one if a person wished to be disabused— admittedly an uncommon predilection. Opinion and dogma, to say nothing of fear and loathing, are much more vivifying and distracting. To the participant shouting at a Nazi rally or the timeserver who has made his or her peace with the gray grief of communism, the attentiveness, honesty, and various splinters of renunciation that are bound to lodge in a lucid soul seem matters of an arcane and hopeless conscience. The beauty of the poets was that a conscience can be both compelling and piquant as it testifies to how imagination can set up shop in the dreariest and most indifferent of circumstances and create quietly remarkable wares. Any place—Maine or Krakow—where an unmitigated conscience is at work is the crux of everything.

The word "conscience" was not one that I encountered in my reading of contemporary American poetry. It clearly was not an academic or stylistic word. It had nothing to do with the literary paraphernalia of personality. On the surface it seemed a bone in the craw of art, a protest on behalf of something most people agreed with already. I knew, for instance, that war, according to conscience, was wrong. It was easy to view "conscience" as a word that savored of the self-righteous, the ponderous, and the humorless. It invited the stifling embraces of sanctimony.

One of the startling traits of the Polish poets was how un-sanctimonious they were. They invited no awed hushes as they entered the precincts of art. They did not preen themselves or proffer a false, winning heartiness. They rejected cleverness out of hand. Rather, they evinced various degrees of the confusion and bemusement that are natural to human beings but that poems, in reaching for some imagist *aperçu*, frequently swept aside. They were reserved but trenchant, ironic but engaged, droll but sober, historical but sensuous, focused but oddly discursive—as if, even as they spoke, they were hearing voices in other rooms. How could they summon up such equilibrium? And how could they avoid what seemed the natural disposition of so much American poetry—to put the narrator's self-involvement at the center of the poem?

What I started to realize from my American vantage point, be it on a dirt road or urban boulevard, was that, in a closed, officious society from which the poet was understandably estranged, the annunciatory inclinations of the self were both ridiculous and pathetic. The self is a kettle of identity; it spouts and rattles its lid as it feels, however blindly, its raw, willful energy. In a society such as the United States where the individual is empowered (however tenuously) to pursue his or her own happiness, the self is a natural correlative. The poet's personal life owns a bottomless appetite as it broadcasts anecdotes, memories, frustrations, longings, and intuitions. There is no such thing as irrelevance. Hollywood is hardly an American accident, for each American can star in his or her own movie. Since happiness (as opposed to contentment) is founded on possibility, fantasy is our natural reality.

What was at work in the Polish poets was starkly different. War, ideology, and the lethal blend of bureaucracy, brutality, censorship, and paranoia that was state communism had humbled the authorial self and made it suspect—not on account of the "bourgeois" element that communists loved to fulminate about but on account of its being overmatched. To take some measure of what had happened to human beings in the twentieth century, more was needed than the anodynes of conventional selfhood, of the poet mounting his or her ego and telling how life seemed to him or her. Immersed as they were in the unhappy river of history, the Poles learned about (in a phrase that is the title of one of Stanislaw Baranczak's books) "breathing under water." Whereas, we, in the West, were able to paddle along on the surface assuming that each of us was at the center of some relatively secure sense of personal importance, the Poles were staring at the systematic mockery of the individual and the social impulses that bring individuals together.

Polish poetry as embodied by the likes of Milosz, Herbert, and Szymborska did not have to happen. History deals all sorts of cards; whether those cards have a hand in producing genuine poets is very chancy. That such poetry had occurred seemed a miracle for which gratitude was appropriate. What I found in the books I brought into our house in the distant Maine woods was a poetry rooted in a passionate wariness, a poetry that approached huge dilemmas at oblique angles, a poetry that refused to make a fuss about poetry's powers and yet trusted those powers implicitly. The personae that the poets deployed—the world-weary yet passionate, skeptical yet religious voice of Milosz; Herbert's Mr. Cogito who managed to be Don Quixote and Sancho Panza in the same character; Szymborska's wonderful aliveness to absurdity and her passion for mundane sanity—were in a different league from the testifying self with which I was familiar in the United States. In their various ways, each poet was unmasking history—not in any declamatory fashion but by means of meditation, wit, and a profound refusal to join the general, contemporary din. They gave recusancy a good name. They exemplified the antidote that poetry could be.

This was not to discredit the poetry being written in my native land, a reasonable amount of which will stand the indifference of time. I had framed my own life on a degree of rejection of what was going on in society at large. Poets in America had become professors. In a society devoted to specialization and knowledge, that was understandable. Spirit has to make all sorts of allowances, covert and otherwise. My feeling for irony, however, was alive to the constant bulletins of importance and stature. You could spend a long time before you found a stranger on the street who could name three contemporary American poets. Americans certainly didn't need poetry in the way the Poles had needed poetry. We had more cocktails of emotional sustenance than we ever could count. How diluted, distracted, or self-serving they were was another story.

To me the Polish poets were heroes—not because of their jumping onto barricades à la 1968—but as people who had dared to challenge the great god of history. They had, after all, choices. They could have chosen the hermetic, the arcane, the willfully difficult, the bromides of an avant-garde that is always on the side of the transgressing angels. They could have drowned themselves in booze and sex. They could have killed themselves as the tremendously talented Tadeusz Borowski had. They could have simply given up. But they didn't.

They had taken history on—not so much its massive, Soviet body but more its wily, invasive shadows. A single event may cast an aftermath that lasts for decades if not centuries. It is a truism that wars don't end when a peace treaty is signed. What happens to those shadows—how they deepen and feint—and how people adapt to them seemed virtually inexhaustible subjects as the poems variously etched and mulled those human accommodations. No judgments were made, for the genius of each poet was to bring to queasy life the manner in which the shiftings and scrapings played out. To be at once lost and assertive was to be human. Even the modulated Milosz shared a fondness for the direct yet unassuming tone—"I sleep a lot and read St. Thomas Aquinas / or *The Death of God* (that's a Protestant book)." Those lines seem symbolic yet very real. Great gulfs of spiritual history are presented offhandedly. One wonders immediately who this "I" is just as one wonders about Mr. Cogito's perceptive blunders or the capacious yet personal (yet anonymous) "I" of Szymborska.

The points of view that the Polish poets embodied were subversively eternal. History had gone up in the smoke of Warsaw and the crematoria, but the aromas lingered and permeated every human shirt. The bland authority of the assertive, individual self was almost a joke in such circumstances. Indeed, in the hands of Herbert and Szymborska it was a joke. For Milosz, who was older, there were the unwieldy wounds of the humanist tragedy and the modern savaging of spirit, of more propagandistic wrong turns than anyone could count. Yet the sun rose, people fell in love, and lemons remained yellow and sour. The perennial qualities demanded their due. Praise, however sly, remained a vital part of the poets' currency.

For an American such as myself who was involved in the very American project of making my life over, the mere acknowledgment of history was problematic. I knew the drill well: history was the servant of progress. It testified to where we came from much as a footnote testifies to a source. It was a tableau—mute, movable, and impotent. Even its screams and agonies confirmed maxims of improvement that could be waved like brisk flags. In the present moment, there was no residual pain. If we doted on history, it was because of its inherently puny stature. We patted its simple head because we must move on. When we visited the past, it was more often than not as a theme park, a place where entertainment condescended to reality. We refused to be haunted (which meant, in a sense, we refused to be human). The whole point of leaving another land behind was to abandon history, to exchange the collective lethargy of dynasties for the individual dynamic of the personal. Like a dog, America wanted to follow its unwary, vigorous nose. Groups like the American Indians and African Americans, whose lives had been scarred for generations by outright violence and hatred, were advised to look on the sunny side.

I, who came from nowhere (neither side of my family remem-

bered much about Europe or wanted to remember much of anything) and lived in the seasonal present with the pine trees and
purple finches, had such a nose. Perhaps it was little wonder that
I could not get enough of the deliberate, nervy joy that vibrated
through Milosz, Herbert, and Szymborska. They knew how appalling human behavior could be. They did not wince, but they did not
become unfeeling. On the contrary, as artists, they thrived. They
had been pushed, but they had pushed back—adroitly.

Virtually every day that we lived in our house in the woods, Janet
and I went for a walk. The most purposeful of these was to the
mailbox that stood a half mile away in front of Stanton and Ella's
house. Our road, with its washouts and cave-ins, was more than the
United States Postal Service wanted to deal with. Who could blame
them? The so-called "good" roads could be an adventure. As it was,
our walk was a chance to consider the state of the road in various
seasons: a culvert needed to be dug out or a branch had fallen and
was snagging the flow of water in the ditch. We looked at the road
with an attentiveness that was part anxiety and part commonsense.
Though the town maintained the road in sporadic fashion, it was
our road and up to us to notice what was happening. If we could
prevent a washout, that was worth doing because there was no telling when the town, in the person of the de facto road commissioner
who, among other things, ran a garage, plowed the roads in winter,
dickered in woodlots, and did backhoe work, would throw some
gravel on it.

The road was lined with trees on both sides, including some dying
maples that Stanton still tapped for maple syrup. On the south side of
the road stood Stanton's fields. They were thin and wet. The upper
field opposite our house was growing up in juniper, alder, and popple and had to be bushhogged every other summer. It was hard to
believe these fields had ever been good for much. They seemed rep-
resentative of land that was farmed for a time and then abandoned
as the American West—Ohio, Iowa, or Oregon—beckoned. These

acres were not the prized, relatively rich bottomlands ("intervale" as New England termed it) that were still farmed; the kind of care that might have improved them was beyond Stanton's ken and interest. A farmer who raised beef cattle in the neighboring town had fenced a portion of the land for pasture. The grass was sparse and confused with daisies and black-eyed Susans, but it was something.

In the warmer months, the cows might be congregating under the long, luxuriant branches of the pasture pines, lolling by the little, silted pond, or simply standing there and chewing in that somnolent way of cows that seems the epitome of both dullness and calm. They regarded us with placid, large eyes. What did we, as humans, know? Any creature that hurried seemed idiotic and unappreciative of life compared to the slow grandeur of cows. Our ever-changing, kaleidoscopic motives were delusions. Our aims and imperatives were made up. I often stood and watched them as they went about their unfeigned lives. A calf gamboled; another received attentive licks from its mother; an older cow sampled the salt block; another cow ambled toward the pond but then stopped and stood stock still. What had happened? My vaunting, human knowledge was never going to tell me that one. The divide between animals and humans was a chasm no legend could heal. To take their being for granted seemed a pitiful arrogance.

The upper part of the road's south side was notable for a large bank that cast a plentiful amount of shade. Stanton had told us our road would never be a real road because of that bank. "Who ever heard of a road with a bank like that?" he asked. We hadn't, but then, before we came to Somerset County, we had barely even seen a dirt road. We were poor ones to ask. That our road didn't meet standard highway specifications was okay with us. Having spent time with the uniformity of asphalt, we relished any scrap of difference. The road wasn't on the earth; it was the earth. There was no division. We took what we were given.

The bank began at a bend that you couldn't see around. It wasn't hard to imagine what would happen if a pulp truck loaded with logs came around it as we were coming up. Over the years, various woodcutters worked in the woods beyond our house and, par-

ticularly in the winter when the road was frozen, would take huge
trucks up our narrow road. "Indifferent" would have been a mild
word for their attitude about our dependence on the road. The
world was theirs to stave up—be it woods or roads. They worked
hard; the right to destroy was the least they had coming to them.
Rounding the bend, whichever one of us was driving tended to
pause and prepare to lurch into the ditch on the north side of the
road if a truck was coming at us. Heading downhill on a snow-
packed road, that truck could not have stopped. The close calls we
had left us breathing out slowly and deeply, our mouths sour and
dry. The truck headed on to the mill. Time was money.

The mailbox to which we walked typically contained an advertising circular, a personal letter (Janet and I were both letter writers),
and a bill or two—car insurance or a mortgage payment notice, but
no electric bill or satellite dish subscription. Some days I received
a rejection notice from some journal to which I had sent poems.
If Janet was with me, I stuffed it in a pocket. I was glad to be with
her—why spoil a walk by making her a party to my insufficiencies?
I thought about them enough as it was. I was with someone I loved;
our strolling up and down the road instructed us that every day on
earth was a good day. We were alive. It had taken billions of years
to make this earth. Things were in their sensible places while life
throbbed—"a leaf of grass is no less than the journey-work of the
stars," as Walt Whitman wrote. Complaints, however understandable, smacked of idleness and the knife's edge of conceit.

Not that every walk was blissful. What we brought to the woods
was our own ill karma—the deep uncertainties and confusions
engendered from being wandering Jews who weren't particularly
comfortable around Jews. Members of my wife's family were glad to
remind us that when they (whoever "they" might be) round up the
Jews, you'll be rounded up, too. Such admonitory wisdom wasn't
much help. We were trying to find the ground under our feet, but
our heads were aware of the long, persecuting past. Though "freedom" is a much-bruited word, the openness of America is perplexing
and scary. Self-definition is a dicey endeavor when one is operating
on a few intense but very random glimmers of intuition. We craved

a rural life—that was our nugget of feeling. And were we prepared for the work? For the solitude that often made us feel that we were alone on the earth? For the very different people who lived in the country? For the lack of urbanity that had been our life's blood? For the effects that growing up in rough-hewn circumstances would have on our children?

We walked and talked. Our talking was like a lot of talking—inconclusive but necessary. We tried to figure out what we were doing and how we felt. There were days when we felt terrible—trapped and bewildered. Like children lost in the forest, we asked ourselves how we had gotten here. What answered was the ruminative, forest silence. We loved that silence, but nature rapture did not run in our skeptical blood. As Jews we had been outsiders forever. Our forebears had gone through the bittersweet paroxysms of assimilation, and we were the free-to-choose products. Although the Lower East Side was in us, it was of the long ago. Our fabled American luck had left us on our own. That seemed how American luck worked. You could rue its rootless charm as much as you wanted and seek in your imagination some Golden Age of stability, but we knew we fit the restless, I'm-not-staying-in-the-town-I-grew-up-in profile as much as anyone. Ironic and anachronistic as the term might seem, we were pioneers. We were also molecules of the mass society. We felt that, too.

What woke us up from our discussions was the scene around us. The stream that was a few hundred yards from the house flowed, the wind blew, cicadas vibrated, a woodpecker hammered. We paused, looked about, and listened. We scrambled down the side of a ravine to be near the water. Even the trickle of late summer was bewitching. The thin fan of water spooling over the rocks, the light as it pierced the dark water and was reflected back, the coolness of the tree-shaded declivity, the scattering of lady-ferns here and sensitive ferns there—none of this cared about our mental heat. Time seemed to empty out. Our confusions grew abashed; each step toward home had a contentment that resembled—despite the ache of self-awareness—a storybook. We had happened upon a little kingdom that constituted more earth than we ever could fathom. We had not been banished or threatened. We could live there. In the failing, late afternoon, tree-filtered light we felt that mysterious calm that was peace.

⁂

Our water supply was primitive (a pitcher pump in the kitchen and a piston pump outside, both operated by an obliging human arm), as was our water outlet system (a drain from the kitchen sink into a dry well built of cinderblocks and covered with planks). We had only a small generator for backup power (used mainly to run an electric iron, a Skil saw for the occasional, large-scale carpentry job, and a blender that we used for pureeing soups and making smoothies). A washer and dryer were far beyond such a modest estate. Our laundry capabilities went no further than a clothesline strung between two maple trees and a wooden rack made of dowels on which Janet dried sweaters that she washed as part of spring cleaning.

Hence the Ritual of the Laundromat. Once a week we sorted clothes into several wooden baskets (we would never use a plastic basket), loaded them into the back of whatever Subaru we had at the time, and drove fifteen or so miles to whatever town we had triangulated for the purposes of the errands we had to run while doing the laundry. When you lived far out in the country, you became very organized about your errands, because nothing was convenient. There was Mac's store, which was the center of the milk-gas-beer universe—handy but definitely limited. To get our sorts of essentials—brown rice, wicks for kerosene lamps, leathers for the pitcher pump, organic raisins—we had to go further afield.

It's hard to say how much time I have spent sitting in Laundromats. I could have compiled a guide to the Laundromats of central Maine, but that wouldn't be in the same league as ranking restaurants in Manhattan. Still, there were issues to gauge. One place played a television nonstop. Milosz's line that hell is a place where the tele-screens are never turned off has come true. How did a populace that once chewed on the hardtack of theology come to need the blather of television in public places? Perhaps television had emptied the people, leaving only blank stares. I lost myself in printed depths while some android droned, emoted, squealed, or pitched endless products. I wondered if Benjamin Franklin foresaw the sensate deadening that relentless commercialism would create. Probably not, I decided. He was coming out of the long, medieval tunnel and standing in the broad, eager light of mobile individualism. Who could blame him for talk shows or a car dealer lustily announcing himself as "Jolly John?" I tried to imagine Ben adjusting his wig for the television cameras. Decorum had taken a powder.

Another place had no television (a plus) but too few working dryers. People queued up their carts and passed the time complaining about bad dryers, bad cars, bad weather, and bad luck. In that particular Laundromat a dryer could stay broken for weeks. As a habitual user of personification, I felt sorry for the dryer—doomed to the anguish of inutility. Another place was dingy. The floor had not been washed in years. You might as well dip an undershirt in coal dust as drop it onto that floor. Another place had no attendant on the premises. If a machine broke, you were out of luck. People passed on tips about machines to one another: "Number Six Dryer is Cold Air City"; "That washing machine will spin all day and never stop." More than once I encountered a sign some forthright soul had placed on a machine that simply read "Broke." The word echoed for all of us as we scrutinized our quarters and wondered whether, given the size of the load, we could get the drying done with two or three of them. We Laundromat-ites shelled out enough in a year or two to buy a washing machine, but we rented, needed the money for a car repair, couldn't be bothered, moved frequently—or lived eccentrically.

I sat and looked at people as they looked at me—aging hippie, not a native, sticks his nose in a book. There were the older guys who plainly lacked a woman in their lives. Some of them gave off an unmistakable whiff of truculence—they had foresworn women (or vice-versa) and were glad of it. They had had too many arguments, one-night stands, and pointless phone calls. Everything that was summed up in the equivocal, stilted word "relationship" ticked them off. A Laundromat was a woman's place; they didn't belong there. As they shoved and pushed unruly jeans and shirts into machines, their movements confirmed their resentment. They had suffered too many female-associated indignities. The word "bitch" was never far from their tongues.

From other men came the frayed scent of pathos. They seemed in their work clothes comically inept as they tried to ponder the mysteries of light and dark loads and fabric softener. They may have been doing this for decades but seemed hopelessly naïve and vulnerable. Where was the woman who could do this with bright efficiency and good cheer, the woman who was undaunted by the specter of remorseless dirt? Sometimes one such man would idly pull off his ball cap and permit himself a sigh. Life had let him down—or never picked him up.

There were young women with squalling children. "Fay Anne get down from that table! Fay Anne don't put that in your mouth! Fay Anne mind your mother! Fay Anne you already had candy today!" Chubby little Fay Anne continued to frolic as best she could. The mothers looked at their brats with a mixture of fondness and loathing. All the rural proverbs I heard about the acorn not dropping far from the tree seemed true. Genetics was destiny. Chances were that I had an older sister of Fay Anne's as a student in the school where I worked. She had a hard time keeping the boys away. Sexual accidents that resulted in a new Fay Anne occurred with something like regularity.

There were single women who folded each article upon removing it from the dryer. They moved methodically and calmly. This gesture impressed me as the height of rational caring. It was contemplative yet brisk. Although they had been reduced to cleaning their private garments in a public place, they still had the self-respect to attend to their clothes in the most deliberate fashion. Whatever touches your skin is, in its way, precious. Residues of feeling adhere to even the most modest scraps of cloth. Some days I could have cried watching these women. I always threw our clothes into the basket or laundry bag and did the folding at home. I wanted to flee the hot, stuffy air and sickly, chemical stench. After an hour or so, I felt like human lint.

Yet it was peaceful sitting there with nothing to do but read or prod a stubborn poem while waiting for the family's clothes to be done. There was no hurrying the wash cycle or the drier. I doled out the quarters and listened absently to the dumb whir and hum of the vigilant machines. I picked up my paperback. Complex laundry doer that I was, I had an affinity for writers such as Henry James. Each sentence seemed a portrait so carefully observed that it proposed—but firmly rejected—exhaustion. A paragraph formed the funnel of a well-mannered, verbal cyclone. The orchestrated relentlessness of his verbal obsession daunted and pleased me.

My engagement may have been little more than a higher form of escapism. Skowhegan, Maine, wasn't Paris, Rome, or London. As people around me grunted various monosyllables of semi-communication, the Jamesian penchant for talking in elaborate, complete sentences seemed not so much outmoded as extraterrestrial. What would the Master have made of the buzzing fluorescent lights, the badly worn linoleum, the stray rumpled notices tacked up for collie puppies or child care or seasoned cord wood, the pamphlets left by Jehovah's Witnesses, the glowing pinball machine featuring Double 07 or Charlie's Angels? Henry James had a hard enough time looking at the raw, immigrant America of the early twentieth century. All those marvelous adjectives and discriminations spoke for a more long-standing and rarified air than what passed for oxygen in the Laundromat. He had been a glutton for civilization. Someone did his laundry; someone starched, ironed, folded, and stowed it. I could appreciate that work.

✷

Because they make so little fuss about themselves, it's easy to make a fuss about country people, if not out and out idealize them. The contemporary siren of self-involvement didn't apply to most people I met, people who often worked long, exhausting hours. As they saw it, they were doing what needed to be done. What they thrived on, what they faced each up-before-sunrise morning, was duty; it was almost a pleasure to them. They were Yankees in the classic sense—self-sufficient to a fault and not immune to a quiet contempt for people who complained. The notion of making a to-do about any difficulty appalled them. It was almost as if there were no difficulties. There were only tasks, some more arduous than others, but all of them important in the hardworking scheme of things. The older people, in particular, seemed relics of another, pre-psychological age. In many ways they were.

Although they were high-minded in that they expected a good deal of themselves, they weren't idealists. On the contrary, they pooh-poohed any social engineering scheme as inherently soft-headed. To Stanton, a government program such as Head Start seemed like Bolshevism. Their notions of probity were rigorous. They despised debt; no upright person used a credit card. Anything that was lent to them (and they disliked, of course, to borrow anything in the first place for the obligation it incurred) came back in the same shape it had been in, maybe better. Janet joked that I should lend out my tools more often as a way of getting them sharpened.

They weren't hypocrites either; the high standard to which every-one should be held began with them. This attitude could be hard on human failings, yet it gave some straitened lives a genuine no-bility. If a trait of nobility is lack of envy, then many people I met were noble. To an outsider they might have seemed to be stuck in hard, narrow situations—felling trees, doing piecework in facto-ries, driving long distances to jobs that lacked any trace of glamour or prestige. Yet what I encountered again and again was a strong sense of "this is my life and I wouldn't trade it for anybody's." A cynic might call this outlook a lack of imagination, but I wouldn't agree.

The circumstances, to be sure, were hardly noble. Likely enough, I was talking with a dairy farmer in a barnyard, cow shit on my shoes, my nose full of that assailing odor. Or I was poking around in an attic that hadn't been ventilated in decades and staring with a widow at a sepia photograph of a young man with suspenders and an unruly grin. No one had done anything remarkable in a news-worthy way, but many people had persevered in very trying circum-stances. You learned about how someone's barn had burned down, how someone's wife had fallen asleep at the wheel while driving home from the three to eleven shift, or how someone's son had gotten his hand caught in a corn chopper. You never heard it from the person to whom it had happened—never. People took what life handed out but refused the consolations of dissatisfaction.

The lack of self-consciousness that I encountered over and over had to do, I think, with the sempiternal quality of the country. Those who spend a good deal of time in proximity to the earth are inclined to feel how finite one human ego is. The seasons turn minutely and inexorably, the first snow falls, deer stand at the edge of the far field, the road up to the house gives off a fine dust in the withering heat of summer. The natural world isn't stoic, only indifferent. The human hullabaloo is distant. Self-deprecation comes more easily to those who know how little say they have in large matters. Anyone whose livelihood depends upon the weather is being measured by vaster forces than he or she can ever hope to conjure. You can look at the sky, but telling it what to do is another matter. An understated irony pertains to rural people; the noise of the city amuses them—as if there were something new under the ancient sun. Urban grandees who expect to be treated with deference may be disappointed.

The heart of the country is farming; the ruination of small farms by the forces of the market has been a very sad affair. The grotesquerie of bigness—big farms, big cows, big equipment, big mortgages—speaks for itself. Mass efficiency extracts a mighty human toll. The town I lived in was once mostly farms. When we moved there in the mid-1970s, only a handful of them were still around. Then those few started to go under. That meant, of course, fewer and fewer farmers. That meant fewer and fewer people like Ned Hoskins who had farmed his whole life.

Ned's eighty or so acres were on the Green River Road, a gravel stretch that wound along the little river that ran through the northern half of town. Various old-time but still working pieces of farming equipment stood across from the farmhouse, as did the modestly sized barn. The house could have used a fresh coat of paint. The barn's clapboards had seen better days. Hay fields extended along one side of the road. Ned milked around thirty or so cows. They had names, not numbers.

Ned's venture would be dismissed as a hobby by agri-business, an infinitesimal drop in the economic bucket. It was, however, Ned's life work. He had grown up on the farm. It was what he knew in detail and what he quietly loved. He left high school during his junior year—in an echo to Caleb, "Not much point sittin' there when I could have been workin'"—and stayed on the farm. We learned from others (Ned never would have mentioned it) that his father drank himself to an early, morose death. Ned refused to touch a drop. From an early age he was a man of responsibilities, and it showed. His every movement was careful and slow as if he were considering with his whole body the outcome of any action; an urban friend I once brought to the farm asked me if Ned was a student of tai chi. He practiced a strict economy—nothing went to waste—and he savored each unhurried step. It was from him that we learned something of the beauty of practicality.

The barn declares the farmer; on the outside Ned's was nothing special to look at. On the inside, however, it was a model of neatness. Every tool and implement was in place, clean and honed, and there were lots of them. I had never seen—to choose one item—so many different shovels. Growing up in the city, I had thought there was one all-purpose shovel. Ned had the better part of a dozen shovels for different jobs. They had long handles and short handles, shallow blades, deep blades, square blades, rounded blades, and flattened blades with scoop-like sides. He had a vast chest of bolts that he used to hold together his various machines. They were neatly separated as to size and function. Not labeled, of course. That was all in Ned's head, a head he slyly disparaged in a favorite phrase of his—"dumb as a cow shit farmer."

When I first beheld the stacks of baled hay in the loft, I smiled with delight. I had never seen anything so alive and geometric at the same time. Ned explained to me how the hay had to be kept away from the walls to allow air to circulate. It didn't take much for hay that might not have adequately dried in the field to combust in a hot, tight space. When I stood in the loft and looked at swallows darting in and out, I felt how hard work created a sort of ease. Those bales were not money in the bank. They were the earth's bequest and a man's labor. To regard them was to feel how one action sensibly led to another, how the simplest product took a whole train of those actions.

Ned's milking parlor was small and neat. I often went over with a half-gallon jar that I filled from the holding tank. The milk tasted nothing like what came out of a carton in a store. It was pungent with the smell of cows (what did I expect?) yet also fragrant. Ned told me it smelled different at different times of year according to what the cows were eating. Summer milk was the sweetest. That's why old-fashioned, hand-cranked, summertime ice cream was so good. I had to agree when we made vanilla ice cream on Janet's birthday, the third of July. It was cold ambrosia.

What surprised me about Ned was that, despite his being on the move all day, he had plenty of time to chat. He loved to tease me as to why an educated person such as myself had moved to the country. I had the whole world to choose from—here I was living in a town most people in Maine had never heard of. I told him that was where I wanted to be, somewhere that was more or less off the map. Ned smiled at this and ran a hand over his closely cropped head. It was hard to imagine the things people did of their own free will.

It was often the case on remaining farms that the wife worked a day job for the cash that kept the farm going. Ned's wife, Sue, taught grade school. Whenever I spoke with her, she seemed a bit exasperated with Ned for keeping the farm going. It would have been easier to sell and have Ned use his mechanical ability at a job in a mill. Still, she, too, confessed more than once while we were sitting on the narrow front porch of their house that she loved the farm. She had wanted to raise children there, but they hadn't come.

It wasn't debt that ruined Ned's world, though that didn't help. He got cancer of the throat; the cost and the pain of it were both very hard. He tried to keep his herd going, but he was weakened. There was no one around to help; the days of hired hands were long gone. He knew he had to sell. He knew it all was gone—the International Harvester tractor he tinkered on endlessly, the heft and sweet, dry scent of hay bales, the getting up in the dark morning, making a cup of strong coffee, and sitting in the kitchen for a few, quiet minutes before commencing his chores, the doctoring of calves and chatting with the barn cats. One day while Sue was off teaching, he took his shotgun, inserted the barrel in his mouth, and pulled the trigger.

Such violence ending such a gentle life. His world was a bounded world—the fields, the herd, and the barn were what he cared about. The world at large didn't entice him. A sister offered him a trip to that American Shangri-La, Florida, right after he was diagnosed, but he turned it down. Politics seemed ridiculous to him. He didn't vote in town elections much less national ones. Although Ned literally was a rooted human being, he wasn't some vestige of a simple, rural sage. He loved what he did. I can see his lined, weather-beaten face (he looked a bit like the older W. H. Auden) crease into a soft, crooked smile when I confessed my ignorance of some basic fact of farming. I can see him patting a cow's rump as he sent her out of the barn. "Shittin' and milkin' machines," he joked with me. He didn't mean it.

·※·

Taking care of ourselves the way we did—chopping wood, carrying water, lighting lamps, cooking from scratch, starting fires in stoves—was never a burden or imposition. It was day-in, day-out work, but it was work that had the ring of clear purpose. Split wood and be warm, grow tomatoes and make minestrone, fill the lamps and light them when the sky darkened, keep the outside pump free of ice and draw water for a bath. More than one visitor told us that we were doing nothing more than fooling around, that we were "pretend peasants" in the words of one guest. When I protested that there were no peasants in the United States, that we, too, were citizens pursuing our happiness, she brushed me aside. "You don't have to be doing this," she said.

We didn't, but I didn't have to be writing poems late into the night either. In its Back-to-the-Land way, the household we founded was an attempt to live a poem. Although our path was very different from the imperiously romantic fashion in which Robinson Jeffers in California or D. H. Lawrence in New Mexico lived a poem, I admired how they upheld their living on the earth as a defiantly human gesture that stood in proud contradistinction to the machine-driven world. The artist who makes a virtue of normality and modesty as if making art were one more vocation doesn't really trust art. Art traffics in spirit, and spirit, by definition, is wayward.

It's hard to imagine the likes of Jeffers or Lawrence driving to work and making a paycheck. They were seigneurs who strove to exist on a plane that was at once higher and more primal. Dollars were not going to define them. Our household's economic realities were modest but, nevertheless, real. We didn't have a big mortgage, but we did have one. You couldn't live where we lived and not have at least one car that was in good, running order. When someone spoke disapprovingly about people who lived from one paycheck to another, I held my tongue—that was who we were. For all our manual labor diligence, we were ardent cousins of Jeffers and Lawrence; our life in the woods was an aesthetic economy, an intuition we had for how much beauty lay in both raw and tutored simplicity.

Janet and I never consciously voiced this to one another. It was a premise that governed our decisions and feelings. We were starting over; quite literally, we were building from the ground up. In our way, we wanted to answer the great, unanswered question: "What do these usurpers, Americans, have to do with the land?" Very little around us answered that question. The stores that stood beside roads, the roads themselves, the houses connected by driveways to roads—none of this worked for us. It was too provisional, too arbitrary, too mechanical, too detached. The buildings stood on the ground but not of the ground. We wanted our experience to savor something lengthier and deeper. We wanted to taste the water that came from where we lived rather than the reservoir or holding tank many miles away. We wanted our food to be food we grew, and our warmth to come from trees we cut down. We didn't want to possess the earth, we wanted to be of the earth—a different concern based on a different economy.

Poetry is no stranger to such an economy. As it hooks one syllable onto another, one word to another in a relationship that is at once free and determined, propulsive yet linear, it is an economy in its own right—an ancient one. It is rooted in our steady, artless breath. We get excited, we run fast, we are frightened and hold our breath, we pause and take a deep breath—however dramatic, these actions are natural. Poetry, however, because it builds upon the human pulse, is artful breathing, articulation that plays upon and with the rhythm in our breath. It has that glimmer of self-awareness that distinguishes art and that takes the raw stuff of being, in this case the physical basis of our being alive, and makes it into something else. This something else, be it meter or free verse, bears the impress of breath, the shaping that stems from lips and lungs alike.

This attentiveness underlies poetry's fascination with the economy of language. Since each breath counts, since a breath can't be skipped, since syllables are fitting themselves to breath and breath is fitting itself to syllables, an enormous attention is being paid to the bits of sound that make up words. "Every word matters" is common enough advice for writing anything, but poetry enforces it physically. Poetry breaks the words down into their syllabic components so that it can feel them as raw sound, then offers those sounds reborn, as it were, in lines. An extra word or even extra syllable is a transgression of sorts, a ruining of sensible order, an indulgence, a carelessness, and, worst perhaps, an indifference.

Poetry is a household whose economy instinctively inclines toward harmony. The notion of living in harmony is largely foreign to modern, progressive societies, because harmony implies a degree of stasis that they reject in promoting what is new. Stasis implies stagnation; novelty is dynamism. Traditionally, however, harmony signals something deep-seated to which it is worth attuning oneself. To practice an economy in touch with our breath, which is mirrored in the pulses around us—be they seasonal, animal, avian, insect, environmental, climatic—is to enter a current that is much vaster than the commenting human mind. As passionate practitioners of poetry, Jeffers and Lawrence knew this and delighted in it. Harmonies do exist; they are not phantoms. Our insensitivity and capacity for being distracted do not cancel them out. Aestheticians of all stripes have proclaimed that beauty is harmony. So do the bees in the flower garden.

Santayana once remarked that the pity of the revolutionary, modern world was that it exulted in smashing what once sustained human beings. It should have been weeping. Our lives in the woods came from our weeping and our desire to touch the sources of life that ran deeper than human invention. Poetry, of course, is made up, but because it is a conduit for our varied feelings, it is profoundly natural. When poets get semi-mystical while invoking the importance of breath to poetry, their enthusiasm is understandable. Our breath is our basic harmony and is precious as such. The agony of modern poets is understandable when one reflects upon their awareness of how much was being shattered to make a putatively better world. The persona of a Berryman or Plath struts, brags, preens, and shrieks on the stage that is the poem, but that persona knows that that stage is no substitute for feelings of wholeness, of what Hesiod, thousands of years ago, called "works and days." That persona knows that, although there never was a Golden Age, when we distrust simplicity we distrust our own vitality. Their poetry enacted the misery, pride, and passion of such distrust, of what was once indicated in the word "alienation." Barbed though it was, their poetry tried to break through such distrust.

No one can count all the microcosms at work inside the macrocosms that are the living, breathing world. We sense them, however, and there resides in even the darkest poetry a margin of praise as it honors the rhythmic interplay between breath and language. Similarly, there was in our life in the woods a margin of praise that over decades we came to cherish. The world around us and in us was there. We were not making it up, nor were we trying to fasten it down. Given the fragility of the green world, notions of permanence seemed a desecration of sorts. That fecundity was prodigal, yet that prodigality—all those leaves on all those yearning trees—was an economy. The poets have celebrated this magnanimous economy forever in societies all over the world. The traditional respect accorded poets (odd remnants of which hang on in the modern world) is no sham, for they are devotees and practitioners of harmony. They are people who seek to tune breath, heart, and word to make a pulsating concord.

※

Although my wife and I were both brought up Jewish, the sky god, Jehovah, made little sense to either of us. He was always looking down at the earth, but the distance seemed insurmountable. His compassion felt more like pique. Why had this male god ever involved himself with the earth and its dark riches? How much better it would have been to hover in the desert sky and enjoy the pontifical blankness of the endless air. One understands the longing the desert peoples must have felt for some voice to emanate from that pitiless sky. The stony earth had to be lonely. Yet the portents of that voice often were hectoring, bloody, and weirdly spiteful. If someone is chosen, then a lot of people are going to be un-chosen. If someone is going to be set aside, then a lot of people are not going to be set aside. If someone is going to be special, then a lot of people are going to be un-special. From Genesis on, the Old Testament reeks of revenge and tribal enmities. Little wonder that Jesus came along to try and set things straight (thus creating another dynamic).

"What about the earth?" I wanted to ask my Hebrew school teacher, Mr. Teitelbaum. "And what about it, Baron?" I can hear him saying. His little eyes would be moist with the pleasure of being a vessel, however leaky, of God's celestial words. Even when he ranted (which he often did), he was distant. He'd clutch at his wool knit tie as if it were strangling him. It seemed that divinity had scrambled him. Here he was—a refugee from Nazism—being paid peanuts to teach a bunch of bored, unruly boys who wanted to be outside playing football. What did those ridiculous circumstances have to do with godliness? The Bible might as well have been a comic book to us. But why, I wanted to know even back then as I sat at my desk munching pretzels and staring out a dirty window, was God talking in the first place? What was wrong with silence? Maybe the human race should be listening more carefully and living with the silence. Maybe we could hear our own hearts—or even other hearts. Maybe we could pay more attention to how we lived on the earth and let the sky take care of itself. It didn't seem to need our dubious attention in the first place.

Those "maybe's" led us to our house in the woods where we found ourselves reading in a very different spiritual tradition—Taoism. Reading about Taoism is a contradiction in terms, for the words are meant to take you into the silence inside the words. The trees and rocks and rain were sages, but we weren't used to being with their being. We had noticed them in passing—out of car windows—but we had never lived with them. We sat in the little house as the rain thrummed on the roof and read the very un-biblical words. We paused and listened, paused and listened. Nothing was happening. That was hopeful. Everything was happening.

Taoism's fanciful sanity captivated us, as in the legends of the people who were so content in their own village that they never journeyed to the neighboring one. That example sounded somewhat like where we were living; more than one person considered Boston the misbegotten ends of the earth. We wondered whether that was contentedness or rural indifference to the world beyond one's homestead—or some of both. There was the notion of the Ten Thousand Things and the energy that moved through them. There was the endless play between the male and the female that charged everything. There were the texts, amusing yet shrewd tales in which appearances were upended: a rat outwitted a scholar, a herdsman instructed a painter, a hermit tutored a diplomat in foreign policy. Nothing was as it seemed. The more the human race strained to get it right, the more it got it wrong. When it backed off, it began to realize that effort usually was tainted with willfulness and hence misplaced. To find some human stillness that could be at one with the vibrant stillness of being was the challenge.

We were entranced by Arthur Waley who translated the *Book of the Way* and many Chinese poems. Waley was one of those Brits who followed his own curiosity and struck metaphysical gold. He recognized that there were spiritual traditions that made a great deal of sense that had nothing to do with God in the indifferent sky. He recognized there was art that took part in the flow of natural energy rather than keeping it at a mental distance. He recognized that a small voice could have as much stature as a gigantic voice, perhaps even more. He was a hero to us who needed heroes desperately, not least because the manner in which we lived was bizarre to most people. The questions were always there. How had we gone so astray? What sort of game were we playing? Couldn't we make our peace with the world and content ourselves with the riches of educated irony? Why didn't we respect the engines of progress and want the Next New Thing? And why had we rejected our own spiritual heritage?

Because our time on earth is short, many people want to save up for the next world. The brevity of life is unbearable. They ratify their identity here by trusting that it will be perpetuated in another world. This prospect enables them to live, more or less, in the perishing world. Taoism seemed the opposite of that attitude. It stressed that one should pay attention to what one did in this world, that the sources of life were deep and instructive. There was no shame in our transience. To construct an identity to oppose that transience was, at best, wrongheaded and, at worst, fanatical. To make its points, Taoism favored the tale, a form that, as it approaches parable, abolishes time by divesting circumstances of history. It carries a whiff of eternity as years wither before the pantomime of illustrative actions. The Taoist tales stressed that we should learn by being here each moment rather than cavorting in our heads. The cook who never changes his knife does so because he knows where to place the knife when he cuts. The lute player feels the music in the strings. Everything already is here. If things weren't all here, the human race never would have gotten this far. Our task is to honor, heed, and love the plenitude of energy upon which life rests. Though we distract ourselves endlessly, we are far from endless.

There was great mischief in Taoism, because it refused to respect the social hierarchies of who was important and who was not important. Each person truly perceiving life for him or herself—that is a recipe for anarchy! But it wasn't. In its fashion it bred respect for others, because each person was engaged in learning how deep the well of life was. Unknowing is vaster than knowing, but what of it? Knowing need not be appropriation; it can be an entering that is a yielding. But words start to fail me. One beauty of Taoism was how it honored the physical world, yet recognized all was flux, as if to say, "This is what we have. Do not make too much of it but honor it. You, after all, did not create it, and standing on a Creator's shoulders will be of no benefit. You are little and that is good. Seek to participate rather than to control."

We sat in our house many nights and read the parable-like tales to one another. They delighted us, but they instructed us, too. Perhaps most importantly, they showed us a way—the pun is intended. To feel the sources of life was, at the least, to open the doors of our senses. To open our senses was to learn to pay some degree of attention. I remember coming across moss on a rotted, fallen hemlock. It knew where it wanted to be, and it was thriving, a clean yet deep green that was lush to the touch. Did I know where I wanted to be? That is very hard for any human being. The moss could not speak—but existence is always speaking. Even stones are speaking, for all natural things are among the Ten Thousand Things. Energy is articulate. Every poet believes that. I would never feel all the Ten Thousand Things, but I wanted to feel some of them. To think of the house in the woods as a hermit's cottage in ancient China was pure fancy. I lived now. An automobile was parked in the driveway. But in the wheel of the seasons, I could sense the depth of now. The Way had not vanished. It couldn't.

※

Beyond our house, discontinued roads stretched in three directions. Though farms had once lined them, no one lived there anymore. Two of them were contiguous and formed a snowmobile trail in the winter and, during the rest of the year, a rutted, washed-out corridor for loggers and four-wheelers. The other road branched into a couple of ancient tote roads. Tall grass grew in old ruts; poplar saplings and blackberry canes were everywhere. We could see these former byways disappearing before our eyes.

The Road Washes Out in Spring

We walked the old roads to learn. Initially we knew next to nothing. We could not name a tree or flower or bird beyond the simplest ones—pine, daisy, blue jay. We had field guides to go by; we had our lived-here-forever neighbors to consult. Often the combination of a field guide and Stanton was confusing. Was rock maple the same thing as sugar maple, ironwood the same as hophornbeam, quaking aspen the same as trembling poplar? Was a porcupine the same creature as a hedgehog? What kind of mock orange was it that we dug up from around an old house foundation? It was fragrant, but the ones at the nursery weren't. What sorts of old apple trees were across the road from us? How come tamarack (also known as hackmatack and not to be confused with tacamahac) dropped all its needles in the fall? Wasn't it an evergreen? It looked like an evergreen. Identifying terms grew up like trees in a field—here and there, at once random yet trying to make something like sense. The old-timers laughed and snorted at our books. What, Ella wondered out loud, had the world come to that people needed such things?

We walked on the old roads, in the field across from the house, and in the woods so that we might feel how alive the earth was and how one day was not another. The flow of water in the stream below our house changed from week to week and season to season. Rocks appeared and grew larger as the water went down. In August we could sit where we could barely wade in early spring. We noticed how the trees and shrubs put out new growth in May and June and, by July, had made the buds for next spring. After a few years in the woods, I realized that previously I had never noticed when buds formed. Where had I been? We watched the firs form their diminutive cones. We looked down at scats and tracks and saw what had been on the road the night before—coyote, deer, moose. We paid attention to how galls formed on flowers and fungi on trees, how milkweed went to seed and the wind distributed their gossamer over the fields. We sat and looked at how caterpillars crawled, ants raced about intently, snow fleas formed a black mass on a late winter puddle. We observed Red Admirals, sulphurs, Mourning Cloaks, and swallowtails flutter through the air and then light on wet gravel, clover, vetch, wild roses, or the echinacea in the largest of our flower gardens. We watched them drink—slowly and intently—yet a mere wink of time before they flew off. On the basis of butterflies, you might conclude that existence was inherently poetic.

We also watched swathes of forest be cut down. One tract near us was clear-cut—every single tree regardless of species was taken down. There was slash everywhere, limbs and tops piled haphazardly that resembled the makings of a gargantuan bonfire to appease an angry god. We looked up at the huge skidders that pulled the tree trunks and made enormous gouges in the earth. They seemed like monsters whose intent was indecipherable. Who knew what was on a monster's mind? We heard them starting up in the morning, deep metal groans and labored huffs. We looked down at the discarded plastic jugs of chainsaw oil and motor oil, at the empty bags of potato chips, beef jerky, and cookies. Sometimes we picked up the trash; sometimes we let it sit there. We wondered what happened to the woodpeckers that had nests here or the lairs of hares and foxes. They would move elsewhere, and we knew that. Our tenderness was whimsy; our scruples were a luxury. It didn't put food on anyone's table. Necessity contained not a gram of empathy.

We walked to evoke the feeling of ritual, of doing the same thing over and over yet on a different day. Sometimes we wanted to lose ourselves in the coolness of the late afternoon, when the breeze died down and the birds began to roost. Sometimes we went out at night with a flashlight and walked very slowly, feeling our way over the earth. After a while, we'd turn the flashlight off and breathe in the spectral night. We'd note the fullness or thinness of the moon. We'd read in Eric Sloane that formerly people worked in the light of the full summer moons. What might it have been like to cut hay under a July moon in the last century? The air would have that delicious shiver of the northern summer. (We were closer, after all, to Canada than to Boston.) There would be the green scent of the freshly mown grass. Perhaps an ox or cow would low. People would be talking among themselves about a church social, how a mare had broken a leg and had to be put down, or how someone was getting a spinet for a parlor. Or they would be quiet, working with their scythes and cutters, tedding, raking, bundling, and tossing the hay.

Eventually they would tire and wearily though intently walk back to a house like Ella and Stanton's to go to sleep in their century. Tomorrow's sun would dry the dew off the grass they had cut.

Our walks were the forays of amateurs who exclaimed brightly and returned home keen to search for the name of a bird or moth in the appropriate guidebook. Nomenclature was secondhand lore but lore, nonetheless. Each name we learned grounded us a bit more. It was our pleasure to keep getting excited about the seemingly unexciting world around us. When people from the city asked us, "What do you do around here?" we smiled politely. "We go for walks," we told them, as if imparting some amazing rural news. Sometimes we went on. "Did you know that flickers eat ants?" "Last week we saw a big mass of toad eggs." "The wild oats are out. We found some marsh marigolds, too." "Oh," they would reply in voices poised between quizzical politeness and frank boredom. We let it go at that, but we could have gone on to say that, often when we went for a walk, we wound up standing silently and listening. Maybe we heard the thin hum of a car out on the state highway. Maybe we heard the wind in the trees. To untrained ears, they could sound identical.

❧

On the way to almost anywhere, I was likely to drive by one or another of the wooden, white churches that dotted the villages and towns of central Maine. Whether housing a quieter denomination such as Methodist and Congregational ("Congo" in the religious slang of New England) or a more demonstrative one such as Pentecostal, they testified to the impulse that had led to the founding of New England, the coming of the Gospel to the woods, and the end of the Indians' reign. As buildings they were easy to dismiss. They did not call attention to themselves in the way the typically stone or brick cathedrals of the Catholics did. They were neither massive nor ornate; they did not speak of the one Church. Plain and spare, they testified to the primacy of the inner life and how Protestants had to square their relations with God on their own: no sacraments, no confession, no penance, no elaborate vestments, no hierarchy of priests. That God's spirit resided in such simple structures must have amazed more than one visitor to New England. What churches were these?

In the United States, Protestantism is like air. You don't think about it because it is pervasive. Its vitality, however, should never be underestimated. As recent history demonstrates, its urgency shows no sign of going away; in its fashion, it is perennial. Whether polite or ranting, liberal or reactionary, it remains—a stubborn stake in the land's autochthonous heart. I'm the sort of person who uses "Puritan" as an epithet for whatever repression or hypocrisy is annoying me at the moment, but living in northern New England made the word quietly real to me. Those unassuming churches were not merely integral to the American endeavor, they were the American endeavor.

It was as if what Martin Luther famously started, the United States finished. The notions of freedom and individuality that are so dear to this country, however confused and debased they may be, stem from the Protestant belief in each individual determining his or her own relationship with God. The Reformation was a momentous step for humankind, bringing God and his words down to earth and making Bible-reading individuals responsible for their spiritual well-being. It was audacious, and as much as social and economic mores bury it, the United States remains founded on that audacity. A democracy that believes in each individual's insight and responsibility is an audacious notion. Whenever I sit in a bar and listen to someone after a few beers declare his or her convictions or misadventures (they tend to add up to the same thing), I don't feel I am that far away from a church. Every soul matters; every soul's opinion matters. It's scary, exhilarating, and appalling.

Although hinged on its unwillingness to accept the ways of human sexuality, the dynamic of Catholicism has made sense to me: you err, confess, make penance, receive absolution, err again, confess again. . . . Life stretches out toward eternity in a weary yet tolerable vista of human failing. It's bleak but cozy; it has no great expectations. For those who crave more, who feel a severity and reverence, there is the Church with its vocations and strictures. Most people, of course, are content to follow the pattern or lapse into less-than-ardent attention to the state of their souls. They know the charm is there if they need it. One can always confess.

Protestantism abhors this schema. There is a once-and-for-all quality about Protestantism, particularly in its evangelical manifestations—damned or saved, and that is it. Confession seems small and irrelevant, as is the wheedling guilt that goes with it. The elaborate edifice of logic that sustained the Catholic Church was of little use to the importunate, anxious spirit that wanted to know definitively whether it would be knocking on heaven's door, that wanted to know if it was one of the elect here on earth, that sought a clear sign amid the confusions and temptations. No wonder, as the hand-painted admonitions on the side of more than one Somerset County road testified, some Protestant sects were so taken with the world ending one otherwise unassuming day. What thrill equals apocalypse? It is the ultimate sensationalism. It was as if the great hope of Protestantism, that a human being could form an intimate relationship with God on his or her own, needed to be balanced by an utter lack of hope: people were depraved, and the end was nigh. You better be on the right side. The thought that people could be depraved yet life would nonetheless wobble along was more than could be borne. Luther was vexed by the spectacle of the Church trafficking in spiritual merchandise. Did such depravity have to be? That is the question the United States continues to try to answer as it outlaws liquor or marijuana or seeks to impeach its president for fellatio. Compared to the indictment and attempted abolition of fleshly failings, wars, because they confront a foe of some sort, seem comprehensible (to say nothing of biblical)—murderous political virtue doing its anointed work.

What is deeply modern and deeply American is the ego that lies at the heart of the Protestant attitude. I don't mean "ego" in a selfish way. I mean that the ego is inclined to measure things according to human purposes. Cleaning up the world of human behavior—whether eliminating adultery, smoking grass, or the selling of indulgences—is a human effort (free will being a delight of the devil), and when the endeavor enlists God, it is doing so on the supposition that He would agree. However well meant, it is a radical presumption through which an ironic thread runs: God doesn't measure mankind as much as mankind measures God.

As the home of simultaneous bonhomie—"Have a nice day"—and anxiety—"Where are my pills?"—the United States is the definitive Protestant nation. Mystery is dispensed with, for good nature subdues the ill nature of sin and leaves the individual free to go his or her saved way. God wants to get along with people; the Bible is a trove of quotes posted outside churches for people to read as they pass by in their automobiles. Optimism is not merely tenable but obligatory. The Ten Commandments want to be posted outside the county courthouse; extracts from the Sermon on the Mount are less likely candidates. Focus too hard on human wickedness, as the Puritans did, and you wind up with the anodyne of self-satisfaction. People can only take so much abasement. That is why there is something very winning about the good-natured, bluff earnestness of American Protestantism. God isn't calling for renunciation or asceticism. God is looking for people who are willing to give themselves over to a personal relationship that will guarantee them heaven. As a proselytizing minister who gave me a ride when I was hitchhiking said, "You can't beat that." His face shone like someone with a winning hand in poker.

One difficulty with this outlook is that its purposefulness easily runs amuck: the Puritans had no compunctions about executing their Quaker brethren. We can say that everyone in that era was intolerant. We can point to the horrors of the Inquisition, institutional anti-Semitism, religious warfare, jihads, and on and on. All true, but there seems a permanent ghost in the machine. Missionary, democratic America wants to save the world but has little interest in finding out if the rest of the world wants to be saved. When salvation is the coin of the land, ultimatums come easily. Our reverence for God is printed on our money, something Jesus would find very curious. As patriots, each one of us must testify to our salvation; an outright atheist could never be president.

Each one of us can possess a sort of spiritual capital, a moral surplus rooted in no nonsense assurance. To be saved is to be "all set," in the American colloquial. And what is more virtuous than salvation? A Roman or Chinese philosopher (or American writer such as Nathaniel Hawthorne or Flannery O'Connor) might reply that the pride of salvation easily becomes the ruination of conscience, but that philosopher (or writer) would be of little moment. Unlike Europe, with its legendary dynasties, or indigenous peoples, with their notions of living with the earth as a form of spiritual practice, the nation was founded on the tension between uncertainty—what am I doing with myself in this world and the next one—and utter certainty—God is on my side. It's a powerful concoction.

And not, I hasten to add, all bad. Far from it. My mother's family came here from Russia at the beginning of the twentieth century to escape despotism and persecution. That this polity was founded in part by aristocratic deists remains beside the point. Protestantism helped open the floodgates of individual enterprise and mutual acceptance. That such an enterprise might become trivial, dangerous, and shortsighted goes without saying. That such acceptance might degenerate into the babble of television, into a make-friends-and-influence-people attitude, or into the worship (the word is irresistible) of material progress seems understandable. Protestantism puts a great deal of weight on our frail shoulders as each of us cuts a deal with eternity or walks, limps, staggers, crawls, or runs from the promising yet reproving table. We can be smug, or we can be lost. The middle ground of intent searching and self-appraisal is hard to find and harder to live with. So is its fragile civility. Consider Martin Luther King Jr., a Protestant hero who exemplifies the extraordinary insights that searching may produce. Then consider his fate (and his thick FBI dossier). Little wonder in the face of a martyrdom that cannot be called martyrdom that this nation is the land of Disney. We need the sedative of innocence in the worst way, for it forestalls conscience. Perhaps we should wear our Mickey Mouse caps daily. It would show as well as anything what we yearn to be— adults divested of the anxious weight of adulthood.

The little, unassuming churches continue to beckon. They sit like rough arks on the land of which they never have become a part. Why would they? They are about the dynamic that pushes and pulls us each human day. They testify to the God whose silence is interpreted by our clamor, who is remote yet available, who offers mercy and takes away life so calmly, who is content with a secular world yet demands protestations of virtue and condemnations of vice. Despite their white clapboard blandness, they proffer the most quixotic blend of good fellowship and solitary fear. Who would guess how much spiritual genius resides in those modest signs that adjure the passerby to get with Jesus and eat a chicken dinner next Saturday evening? My wife and I ate some of those church dinners to which we were invited by neighbors or to which we went out of curiosity and hunger. We sat at long folding tables with plastic tablecloths and ate what Yankees consider to be decent chicken, at once tasteless and leathery. People were excruciatingly polite and exceedingly good-natured. I appreciated that. When we said that we weren't interested in going to church on Sunday but just in the dinner, I could feel their inner selves wince. I didn't blame them. Every soul matters. As an American, I couldn't agree more.

※

When, one summer, a well-known poet from New York with whom we had become friends visited us, she exclaimed immediately and at length about our flower gardens. To use her uncommon word, we were "embowered." She oohed and aahed over the phlox, shasta daisies, dahlias, delphinium, mallows, and day lilies that grew in variously shaped beds in front of our house. She confessed that she hadn't expected such a profusion of scents and colors. She hadn't expected to see dozens upon dozens of flowers.

I teased her as to what she had expected. Somewhat sheepishly, she confessed that she thought we were "going to be more utilitarian." She assumed that for us there was no room for the exuberant luxury of flowers. We were water not wine. When I protested that I, like she, was a poet, hardly a utilitarian endeavor by the standards of the practical, get-a-job world, she laughed her wonderful, girlish laugh. Flowers didn't fit her notion of Back-to-the-Land rigor. The pink and white petunias that grew in two window boxes attached to the south side of the house did not fit. Loveliness did not fit.

From the first summer that we lived in the woods we grew scads of flowers. Why we grew flowers wasn't complicated—they were beautiful. Wearied by the sheer ugliness of the manmade landscape, we hungered for beauty we could take in daily, beauty that spoke to both aesthetic and horticultural longings. The clearing we had made among the pines and maples made the blooms that much more piquant; our gardens' mix of orderliness and sprawl existed in bright, swaying, fragile contrast to the stolid woods. The woods, as they grew up from the fields, had happened randomly. The flower gardens hadn't happened randomly; they had been created from nothing and cultivated carefully. As a person walked around and through the gardens, the blend of heights, colors, scents, forms, foliage, and textures made delightful shows. Each year Janet meticulously noted in a journal each plant in each garden and wrote observations for next year's plantings. To use our poet-friend's words, the gardens were "very civilized." One implication of course was that we, as people living off the grid, weren't civilized.

We joked about this with her—had we traded the common amenities for higher ones, or was it vice-versa? For all the digging, fertilizing, staking, snipping, dividing, hoeing, mulching, watering, cleaning out in the fall, storing dahlia tubers over the winter, ordering seeds, growing plants from those seeds in flats, and replanting what had been winter killed, the flowers were sheer joy. What were hard workers doing indulging joy? When we looked around, we saw that we were in step with the older women (definitely not the men) in our rural neighborhood. Ella grew a good hundred feet of gladiolas for the sake of their display in August. She didn't sell them, though she gave plenty away. She loved them dearly. Caleb's wife was proud of her stand of golden glows that bloomed every August in front of their house and that seemed the archetypal, old-time Maine flower. They stood around five-feet tall; their yellow heads were the essence of sun. We transplanted some of them to our gardens.

We noticed that local people who were our ages often had no flowers in front of their recently built houses. It was painful to look at a house and see nothing beyond a mown lawn and a scraggly pine that had been brought in from the woods and left to its own devices. What had happened in a little over a generation's time? To us it seemed that the resourcefulness that the old-timers personified extended to the cultivation of what was beautiful. Beauty wasn't an add-on. It sustained human beings and it mattered. Even curmudgeonly Stanton admitted that Ella's gladiolas were so stunning as to be necessary. It wouldn't be summer without them. For many in the next generation, the satellite dish apparently replaced the burgeoning earth. It did not give them beauty, but it gave them sensations that, however remotely, made them feel alive and in touch with the greater world. Secondhand reality was preferable to firsthand experience.

The flowers existed for their gorgeous, sexual, emphatic selves. The apostrophes to flowers that poets had been writing for millennia made exquisite sense — in its sensual intensity, a poem was a blossom. The lyric impulse honored the showy intensity of our feelings. Like flowers, our feelings required no explanation. They existed as the overflow of spirit. As our poet-friend wandered about the yard exulting about the dahlia colors — salmon pink, plum purple, and white with crimson rays — and their florets — "a honeycomb of tears" — the analogy between poem and flower never seemed more apropos. She pronounced our "bowers" to be "ravishing." I knew that was something she sought in her poems — to delight the reader with the beauty of the physical world. When that day she inscribed in her most recent book that she depended on Baron and Janet "to keep us all honest," we understood all around how beauty was part of that honesty. We made a bouquet for her and set it in a quart canning jar. She applauded both the flowers and the container.

✻

For many years we voted downstairs in the kitchen of the wooden Grange Hall. Then we voted downstairs in the library building when it was refurbished and turned into a proper town office, which is to say when a concrete foundation was put in and a flush installed. The downstairs of the Grange smelled like gingerbread and baked beans. I don't think it had ever been ventilated. The downstairs of the library smelled like air freshener tinged with the scent of M & M's, which the town clerk set out in a little basket as a gesture of welcome. We held town meetings upstairs in the Grange Hall and then, when that got too small, in the elementary school gym/auditorium. We had no town building, though we did have a town library that went back to the nineteenth century and contained numerous relics from the age of literacy such as Hume's *History of England* and the complete works of George Eliot. Neither had been taken out in a long while.

For many years the town had been saving money to build a proper municipal building, but it had mixed feelings about actually doing so. The money the town had set aside was more appealing as a rainy day fund than as going for actual nails and lumber. As befitted local democracy, the town had mixed feelings about most things. It wanted to take care of its historic past, but it didn't want to bother with decrepit buildings. It wanted to affirm rural life but yearned for the amenities of the with-it, electronic world. It wanted to take care of its own business but often was overwhelmed by the demands the state placed upon it. A few tiny towns north of us gave up the organized ghost and disbanded. It was hard to find people to serve as the selectmen and selectwomen. The jobs paid little and, if done in any way close to the letter, took time.

People complained no matter what you did. Many towns polarized around out-of-staters and in-staters. Out-of-staters wanted more oversight, which often meant some form of zoning; in-staters wanted to keep the traditional ways that let people do what they wanted with their land. Out-of-staters tended to be professional types who liked things to look nice. In-staters resented having to kowtow to the notions of people who had grown up in other places and had other, foreign ideas; people had the right to have as many out-of-commission cars in their front yard as they wanted. Out-of-staters might post their land to keep off what they perceived as trigger-happy hunters; in-staters felt that property lines were immaterial when out hunting. The townspeople chewed on these issues for decades but did little. It didn't seem imperative. Jobs were scarce; winters were close to interminable. "This state is on the way to nowhere," a pessimistic speaker from the floor at town meeting once put it.

Town elections and town meeting were held on the first Saturday of March. The first year we lived in town, it snowed the better part of a foot that day. We had parked our car at Ella and Stanton's earlier, then snowshoed the half mile to their place with our daughter in a backpack to get to the meeting. We had to attend town meeting because the warrant had an item about maintaining our road. Maintenance had been discontinued, though no one was sure when or how that officially had happened. Everyone assured us we would be taken care of. Even though it wasn't officially sanctioned, we had been plowed out all winter. After the first storm, we stuck a pint of whiskey in a snow bank to show we were appreciative; the offer was accepted.

At town meeting there were scattered complaints about hippies moving in and making demands on the town, but the item passed overwhelmingly. "Maintenance" turned out to be a pretty loose word anyway. When the road became impassable, the town did enough to make it passable until the next time it became impassable. The longer we lived there and drove around on back roads in other towns, the more blasé we became. Once I was taking a student home in a hamlet thirty or so miles north of us and drove the Subaru through two small streams. When I questioned the student, she said that the town had told her family that the streams went with the road. Culverts cost money the town didn't have.

The cast of selectmen (there were no selectwomen until Janet held the job for a year) changed modestly. Sometimes the selectmen were businessmen who wanted the town to take care of its affairs in a more efficient manner. They argued for rational economies like dispensing with the discount the town offered for paying your property taxes early. To make up for the discount, the town raised the mill rate; so what, they asked, was the point of the whole thing? They always lost this argument. People liked the illusory savings.

Sometimes the selectmen were locals whose families had been in town for a hundred years or more and who treated the town as their preserve. One of these solons was famous for throwing letters from various state agencies into the trash without opening them. "Augusta," he would mutter, as if he were swearing. Sometimes the selectmen were out-of-staters who were progressives and wanted the town to deal with its problems—the dump (later renamed the waste transfer station), recycling, out-of-date bookkeeping practices, land use planning. Typically the whole thing worked cyclically as one group got tired and townspeople got tired of it, so another group came in. In terms of the law of averages, it worked reasonably well.

Town meetings were spectacles that provided an opportunity to muse about the ability of the human race to govern itself. As in a Ben Jonson comedy, there were various types of characters. Taxation looked at all issues in terms of whether the tax bill would go up or down. Native protested that unwanted laws were forcing out local people. Transplant lamented how Maine was turning into the New Jersey that Transplant had fled only a few years ago. Patriot complained that we had fought wars to keep free, and here, right in our own state, bureaucrats were hamstringing us. Save-a-Buck noted that we really didn't need the five streetlights in the village that we paid Central Maine Power for; according to him, no one went out after dark anyway. History lamented our lack of local pride. Futility pointed out that we had debated the same issue last year to no purpose whatsoever. Town meeting was a chance for everyone to speak up. More than once I reflected that the U.S. Senate probably wasn't much different from this. The thought was not comforting.

As newcomers we kept a low profile but were civic. I was on the board of the library for fifteen years and served as treasurer most of the time. We had our meetings on the ground floor of the library, a clapboard building that had been a shop and still had large counters from the nineteenth century. The counters weren't particularly appropriate for a library but were wonderfully atmospheric. I could imagine a clerk laying out a bolt of dimity while discussing whose children had the croup or whether spring would ever come. We had a very modest appropriation from the town and an endowment we watched over carefully. We were open Saturday afternoons. Maine didn't have county libraries. For our town, we were it.

Because we were not shy about receiving donations, our collection was miscellaneous in the extreme. If we excelled in anything it was romances, mysteries, and Westerns. Caleb often showed up to collect a bunch of ragtag Westerns that dated anywhere from the 1920s to the 1950s. He noted cheerfully that he'd read each of them a few times already, but he liked to read them over and over because he still forgot most of the words. In return for the nickname he gave me, I nicknamed Caleb "The Arizona Kid" after one of his favorites, or "Arizona" for short. Since he'd never been west of New York State, he was amused.

The library bought romances from a company that specialized in them. They were hardcovers and invariably featured a dreamy looking woman on the front jacket staring off at something or someone the viewer could not see. She had a hairdo that went out in 1954 and usually wore a cardigan and a blouse with a Peter Pan collar. Maybe there was a circle pin on her blouse. I tried to imagine falling in love with her but failed. Then again, when those prim, pensive lips "melted," it would be an astonishing feeling. Cowboys, detective stories, and love all possessed a formulaic solace. For some members of the community we provided a service.

Janet served as selectwoman for one year. That meant (as was the case with my library position) that she ran for office on a ballot. No one opposed her. It was during the reign of the out-of-state selectmen, so another out-of-stater hardly mattered. Among other responsibilities, she took care of the concealed weapon permits. It was surprising how many people had an interest in walking around armed. Then again, when you thought about the rifle racks in the pickup trucks and the NRA stickers, it wasn't so surprising. Mostly Janet dealt with Stewart, the contractor of sorts who took care of the roads. We didn't have a road commissioner the way most towns did. Stewart was the true boss of the town, because everyone cared about the roads, which meant keeping them passable, plowed out in winter, and in good enough repair for people to avoid large front-end alignment bills. Janet and I put well over thirty thousand miles each year on our cars. If you were rural, you ran the roads.

Stewart was good-hearted, hard-working, and didn't like being told how to do his job. A former Marine, he had seen combat in Korea. He was a savvy businessman who earned a living without leaving the borders of our town. He plowed snow, fixed the roads, did backhoe work, graded building sites, bought and sold wood lots, and operated a garage. Stewart loved to talk and excelled at a sort of mock logic in which he protested his innocence and ignorance at the same time as he expounded about how things should be done. "He was just a country boy, but. . . . He wasn't a Portland lawyer, but. . . . He hadn't been to college, but. . . ." He had a monopoly on the business of roadwork, and he knew where he stood and how to exact the maximum benefit from that position. He was a linch-pin of the town who was ever protesting his honor, as in, "If you don't like how I do the roads, then you can do the roads." Robust but touchy, his honor was a shield that protected him from too close scrutiny. Janet humored him: "Now, Stewart, I know you are bus-ier than a one-armed paper hanger but the Town Farm Road was supposed to be ditched last month." He humored her back: "Now, Janet, don't worry your pretty head about that. We'll get that taken care of before the snow flies. How are you doin' out there in the williwacks? Seen any moose lately?" That was how business got more or less done.

While our various local political comedies and occasional fra-cases transpired (members of an aggrieved faction shot out a few windows in a selectman's house one year), the great nation of which our town was a microscopic part lurched deeper and deeper into the throes of empire. Perhaps it mattered which presidential candidate we checked on the ballots that we dropped into the quaint wooden box, perhaps it didn't. The brutalities that went by the name of *Real-politik* and that testified to what a fraught place the arena of nations was weren't going to vanish because someone who kept up on world events wished it were kinder. Neither the CIA, the Defense De-partment (which took increasingly unbelievable amounts of money for weapons it was ghastly to imagine), nor the huge corporations that instructed the government about how they wanted to do business were going away. The nation's fears concerning national security weren't going away either. When the enemy, communism, with which I grew up, did go away, the political climate did not change especially. One of Caleb's adages was that, if you had big feet, someone was bound to step on them. Someone else would become the enemy and come after us in some fashion. And they did.

The honest response might have been to leave the United States and go some place that wasn't helping despots torture and murder peasants in the putative name of democracy. Those countries weren't existentially better places than this one. They weren't, however, powers of the caliber we were, nor did they have the imperial, missionary blinders we had. The Tao suggested that the way to live was to be pliant. Internally, the heterogeneous United States attempted that pliancy as people tried to coexist. Those attempts to accept diverse humanity were commendable. Schooled though they were in the halting ways of wariness, rural Mainers were reasonably accommodating to us and various others (hippies, for instance, living in communes with alliterative names like Sunny Street and Camp Catastrophe) who started showing up in the late sixties. They practiced a degree of reserve and assumed others would practice a degree of reserve in their turn. A notion of inviolable inwardness still lingered—the Puritan version of live and let live.

Regarding the rest of the world, however, the United States seemed to assume that everyone wanted to be who we were. God had blessed us; everybody else should get out of the way of our invariably good intentions. To us rustics driving gingerly down a corduroy, dirt road in first gear and wondering who would run for selectmen that year, the super-powerful, secretive nation seemed a very distant dream. A handful of people in town flew the American flag. Some of my students went into the Armed Forces each year and wound up visiting places they never would have seen. Stewart raised the Marine Corps flag outside his garage. He reminisced to us sometimes about Korea and how cold it had been. "You think it's cold here. Go sit in a foxhole in Korea in the middle of winter." We listened. Stewart knew incontestably that there was a world beyond our town. That was why he lived here.

※

Once upon a time, when busy-ness was not so much upon the human race, people visited with one another to chat and have a cup of tea. The practice still lingered in the country among the older people. It wasn't that they weren't active. On the contrary, I got tired merely contemplating what an Ella or a Caleb did in a day. They rose early, and they were "at it" (as Ella liked to say) all day long. Nonetheless, there was time to receive company. Among the busiest and the most welcoming was Thomas, a retired Navy man who lived on the other side of town.

Our town was Thomas's ancestral home. His "people," as he put it, had lived in town for generations. They were farmers and small-time merchants who bequeathed Thomas an old farmhouse with over a hundred acres. Thomas had gone into the Navy in World War II, had liked it, and had stayed. He was a spry man, orderly and methodical yet spirited; the term "ship shape" would have described his approach to life. When he retired he moved back to town and the house that had been empty for some years. His military benefits were ample for his needs; he proceeded to improve his place.

Thomas was a natural Jeffersonian—a type one fears is becoming extinct. He believed as an article of faith in small farmers as the backbone of the United States, as people who paid close attention to their land and their farming techniques, and as people who were accountable for how they treated the earth. Like Jefferson, Thomas liked to tinker, coming up with new ways of doing things and trying them out. He had an orchard that he was forever tending—either grafting, mulching, mowing, or pruning. He knew the names of countless apple varieties and talked about them as if they were human beings. As far as he was concerned, they were. "Now a Northern Spy wouldn't do that," he would say in reference to how an apple grew or ripened or was susceptible to scab or worms. Sometimes I almost felt that the apple in his freckled hand would start talking back.

For Thomas each day was an invitation to work with the natural world. This did not stop during the long winter; he had to be out-side daily, not only clearing his driveway of snow but also walking around on snowshoes to keep an eye on his apple trees. When a limb broke in a wind or from snow or ice, Thomas made a note of it for spring. He knew a good deal of poetry and could quote from Frost's poem about apple trees, "Good-by and Keep Cold": "Good-by and keep cold. / Dread fifty above more than fifty below." "That's good advice," Thomas would say. "A warm wind gets that sap moving. Then a cold wind comes and snaps that young tree right in its heart. That man was a poet but he knew something. He wasn't one of those bunch-of-words fellows. No, sirree, that man knew his apple trees." Once, half-jokingly, Thomas confided to me that he preferred Frost to the Bible. "He makes more sense any day." He winked.

Townspeople considered Thomas something of a radical. He cer-tainly held opinions that didn't conform to the notion of a retired military man. He liked, for instance, to hold up the hippies as an example of how people should live. "They got an interest in the earth. That's good," he would say. "Someone better have an inter-est in the earth in this country. There's not going to be any country if we don't wake up. We're lucky to have these hippies." Typically Thomas would be holding forth at Mac's store in the morning. A clean liver, he didn't drink coffee much less alcohol. He bought the local paper each day at Mac's and read it thoroughly. He wrote let-ters to the editor about the government forcing the small farmer out of business. He went to meetings in Augusta and testified before various committees that oversaw agriculture. He was a stellar mem-ber of the Grange and helped plant trees on our town's little strip of public land. He was a citizen.

The world had gone soft according to Thomas. People no lon-ger knew what to do with themselves because they had no chores: no wood to split or cows to milk or chickens to feed or bread to bake. He had no use for television and lamented how much time his wife spent in front of it watching game shows and soap operas.

She had moved from a big city on the West Coast; the adjustment to small town life couldn't have been easy. Shopping, rather than apple trees, was her thing. She and Thomas bickered in the semi-good-natured way of long-married couples. When I talked with her, she usually turned the conversation to the weather and how cold it got in the winter. It seemed a personal affront to her. She liked to recall the "regal" palm trees of southern California. Her brown eyes got dreamy. Thomas, of course, loved the adversity of winter. It was one reason he retired to Maine. "Winter keeps you clear-headed," he would say. Sunny southern California was pleasant but didn't do much for human character.

Thomas's voice was high-pitched, with an occasionally querulous edge to it. He knew that what he loved had largely disappeared. The increasingly shrill, electronic society (it would be hard to imagine Thomas on a cell phone) had passed him and his orchard by. It made for a lingering dissonance in him, a sort of exasperated cheer. He'd seen his share of hair-raising moments during World War II, including being on a ship that was torpedoed. "You wouldn't believe something that big could sink," he told me. "You just wouldn't believe it until you saw it happen." He'd been in a lifeboat that was strafed. "They missed," he said wryly. He was a patriot of an old school—that of American idealism and the notion that contact with the soil made us better people. He hadn't fought for his country so that it could become an endless store. He rued and deplored the paving over of America. Meanwhile, he tended his trees. To use his own word, he "sputtered."

Most young people who grew up where we lived left for better opportunities elsewhere. We had come there because it was a left behind, unnoticed place. Thomas was alive to that irony. He delighted in how we lived and our interest in the old ways. He once pronounced us "the new old-timers." We walked through abandoned orchards with him as he told us about the trees, how they had been grafted, and the sorts of apples they once had produced. In the nineteenth century our town had shipped apples to England. They kept through the winter and were sold in the early spring. However modest it was, we had stood for something in the annals of pomiculture. Now we were woods and quasi-suburbs—vinyl-sided houses with lawns that called for large riding mowers. It was a comedown from the former vigor of farm life in a nation that didn't tolerate comedowns. Though he was a bundle of ameliorative energy, what had been lost haunted Thomas.

If it isn't simple-minded, optimism is a terrible strain. Thomas tried to be a good-natured gadfly; he mostly succeeded. He would have been the first to say that he would have been happier in an earlier century. The thuggish manners and technological insouciance of the late twentieth century didn't amuse him. He didn't want to be entertained. Gladly he took on the burdens of rural work. It was said of him, as was said of us, that he was only playing, that he was a gentleman farmer who was living quite well off his pension. To make that criticism was to slight the vision that impelled his days, a vision that those who preferred shopping malls to apple orchards dismissed as outdated and irrelevant. "Every tree is peculiar," he liked to say when discussing how apple trees developed and bore fruit. There was something precious in that view, something that honored intractable, earthbound, individual energies, something nurturing and attentive that looked carefully at insects, leaves, and soil each day. As a person slowly walked around a fruit tree and considered which branches to favor and which to cut, the task of pruning was as good a model as any for the deliberation that we might bring to life. Heedlessness was not a virtue, and Thomas believed in virtue. If we didn't pay attention to what the natural world was telling us, we were fools. Anyone who asked Thomas about global warming would get an earful.

There must have been many men and women like Thomas during the settling of the nation by the white people. They must have been restless and intense as prophets, people who never stopped trying to improve their land and their situations. They were shortsighted, full of hopes, and deluded. They also were unwavering, visionary, and filled with a commonsense that was a first cousin to wisdom. When Thomas saw some apple trees trying to hold on in the midst of what now were woods, he would make a thin, clicking noise with his tongue against his teeth. He was scolding the race that had abandoned what it had started, that left so much to oblivion.

✻

One comment people in rural areas often make is that the country is a good place to raise children. That's a comment that I've also heard parents make about suburbs, good-sized towns, and, for that matter, metropolises. Allowing for human partiality, a special claim for a rural upbringing is understandable. The green and dreamy tableau of a bucolic childhood, one steeped in the sensations of the natural world, exerts a powerful attraction. Despite the depredations of psychological insight, to say nothing of observing how children bully and berate one another, childhood is a precious, brief, and, at least in the earliest years, unvarnished existence. We come into the world with an agenda of predisposing genes and appetites, but we also come with the sensory equipment to respond to the extraordinary pageant that we summarily call "life." The spectacle of a child watching a turtle, salamander, or bumblebee is beguiling and vivifying. That the unmediated impressionism of childhood should be one of the touchstones of Romantic poetry makes good sense. That quickness of perception, unhampered by the brittle, defensive wiles of knowing, seems a blessing. The notion of childhood as paradisiacal, however contaminated that notion is by adult, wishful thinking, has a grain of truth in it. For a time, mind and experience have yet to overwhelm existence; becoming has not suborned being. The assertive drone of identity has yet to surface.

"His day is a dawn," I wrote in a poem about our son; that was true for both our children when they were small. From the perspective of adulthood, it is easy to dismiss childhood as the tail of a human life. It is what is left behind. How it informs the world of grown-ups is mysterious and capable of endless unraveling that may or may not please the probing adult. Childhood has no answers; it is about receptivity, about taking in the myriad shows of existence. Although we think of childhood as foundational, it has a life of its own. It is the lyric pulse that dwells within poetry; it is the sheer, undetermined fact of being alive. We often are eager to trace our debilities to our parents' shortcomings; usually there are more than enough of those to go around, sometimes much worse behavior than flaws of character. We see our adult selves as stories stemming for better and worse from those sources. Yet the fey, beckoning intensity of childhood remains. Explanation is not the charm of childhood.

We brought to parenthood a common enough determination—not to do to our children what had been done to us. Neither my wife nor I were whipped or seriously threatened as children. It was more the indifference to who we were on the inside that rankled us, those endless days spent dealing with adult expectations of who we should be that were based on who our parents wanted us to be. Our parents were hardly the first to be wary of children who displayed artistic leanings. Although my mom encouraged my writing when I was a teenager, she made it plain that becoming a writer as an adult would be irresponsible in the extreme. My dad, an accountant, thought accounting was a good idea. For Janet, a child who liked to paint and draw, art school was never a consideration. To put one's own predilections about earning a living onto one's children seems an understandable, if anxious, parental prerogative. To do otherwise takes a degree of imagination and faith. Both those qualities may be synonyms for fond folly, panning that wistful gold called "potential."

The extremity of our life in the woods spoke to the extremity inside us. Since Janet and I found mass life at once dreary and frenetic, we decided we would try to lead manifestly individual lives. We would reclaim ourselves as we reestablished contact with our parcel of the pine needle earth. We were for purity and directness of experience, mindfulness made vivid by the spontaneity of nature's moods. Our children would eat food that we grew and play on land we took care of. They would go to bed in the lap of the dark woods and wake to the light hallooing through a window. When your nearest neighbor lives a half mile away and your house is a thousand or so feet from a dead-end road that practically no one ever drives on anyway, you don't need curtains, blinds, or shades. Exasperated by our parents' generation that practiced repression as a form of social wisdom (the tireless litany of Don't Do That) and that avoided the body's unruly imperatives as much as possible, we chose nakedness, both literally and figuratively.

Clothed as we were for winter a good deal of the time, swaddled in scarves and sweaters, those moments in the summer when we cooled off under the outside pump—deep, granite-cold water— were especially lyric; the shouting, tingling interstices, the ecstatic rushes that made us feel how alive our flesh was. We knew that a whole life could not be fashioned out of such rapt occasions. We also knew that people were prone to push the lyric moment aside as an unwanted reminder of how sweet life could be. Dutifully they buried it in photographs that were records, reminders, and signs of feelings. It was as if they went on vacations for the sake of their cameras. They allowed themselves a time-out to feel. In my mind's eye, I see my mom trying to smile in a photograph taken by the Pacific Ocean. She's going to die within the year. The doctors have told her that they can't do anything more about her cancer. She had always wanted to go to California. California is Eden, and if, like the original, it's gone wrong, it still has a florid, heady scent. She's got this half-cocked, loopy grimace of a smile. She's palpably sick, but she's alive at that moment. That's good enough. It should always be good enough. A real, dear smile is our inner nakedness, the simple love that spends most of its fugitive time on earth hiding. My mom knew that the camera was a grave.

Out of the moments we construct stories, those approximations that speak to skeins of feeling—grudges, desires, memories, shames, frustrations, obsessions, losses—the list is endless but doesn't include love. Love is not continuous. Affection may be continuous—a good habit that sustains the spirit—but love needs the kindling of moments. It's not hard to be greedy for those moments; the bleating schlock on the radio knows that much. I don't think of our life in the woods as greedy but more like kismet, more like creating a chance for the moments to occur, more like an invitation on the part of the unwitting but willing spirit. When I read about people who worshipped the sun or the moon or trees, it made more than a modicum of sense to me. What were we doing if we weren't in some capacity offering up our awe? The mantra we took from the on-going moments was that none of this extraordinary and sustaining display has to be. However slowly and intermittently, we started to feel that.

Childhood is founded on awe—that's why leaving childhood is so bittersweet. The lure of adulthood is powerful and physical, but the intuitions left behind have the haunting, asexual glimmer of timelessness. Our children learned to swim in a pond nearby, and I can see their efforts, full of determination and a dash of fear. They learned to bicycle on the dirt road in front of the house. Soon they were going down the little hill with an echoing whoop. In winter they sledded down that hill on wooden sleds and shouted with quick joy. They played Little House on the Prairie in a ramshackle playhouse I built from scrap lumber. Their childhood lives were solitary. No playgroups were on their schedules; they had no schedules.

When they went off to school, it felt like a scintillating exile: *there is a bigger world.* Decades later when I think about what their expectations about school must have been and what they encountered, it still saddens me. The local schoolhouse that contained three grades wasn't a much bigger world. It was big enough, however, to have children who threw tantrums, fought, bragged, lied, and taunted. That was nothing unusual—they had their own unhappiness to act out—but it was new to our children. They came back each afternoon to the house in the woods and wondered about how insensitive some people could be. They wanted to fit in, but it wasn't going to be easy. In creating a world we had, in a sense, cast them out.

I rued their confusion. Who cared for the exclaiming, second by second, chancy authenticity that meant so much to their parents—the mere wind in the mere trees? Janet and I lived our lives in our alert skins but had no firm, long answers. We worked hard but were quixotic. Our children trusted us, as children do. We strove to show them despite our own dilemmas that something precious was at work during these moments on the earth. It was something that couldn't be bought, sold, judged, or even talked about very much. It had nothing to do with the spiels of socialization that made life approximately comfortable. It was real though. When I overheard them acting out Laura and Almanzo in their playhouse, I had the uncanny feeling that these two children were apprehending other, long-ago lives in the present tense of their own lives. It was a poignant, almost unbelievable moment. "I don't know if I've ever seen such a snow," Maisie said. "Well, that's how it is where we live," Owen replied in a grave voice. Perhaps because the gifts of imagination are bottomless, we human beings have a hard time acknowledging them.

∗

Our children grew up during the presidency of Ronald Reagan. On the school bus they sang to the tune of "Frères Jacques": "Marijuana, marijuana, LSD, LSD / Ronald Reagan makes it / Howard Parker [the school bus driver] takes it / Why can't we, why can't we?" Somehow what's sung on school buses never gets into the official annals. The official annals record that America was told to "just say no." I tell writing students to keep a sharp eye out for the rhetorical trap that lies in words such as "just," words that seek to insinuate more sense than is actually there. Such words can be overbearing and evasive at the same time. After all, how the U.S.A. was supposed to summon the will power to do that nay saying wasn't answered. Nor was it explained what America was saying "no" to, beyond the usual fears propagated in the newspapers and on the television. What it might say "yes" to was also left out. Shopping? Investing? Watching more television? Why it was wrong to smoke marijuana to deal with anxiety but okay to take a Valium never got on the docket either. It may have been that the kids on the school bus enjoyed the naughty parody they were performing without giving it a second thought. It may have been that they intuited the emotional chicanery at work in the breezy, powerful, yet nervous nation. Kids have a nose for a society's hypocrisies and fears. What adults parade as reasons may seem to young people as so many authoritarian assertions based on dogma and uneasiness—a bad combination that often goes together.

What did it mean to live for eight years with a president who was so patently a performer? For many people, it was fine and dandy, acey-deucy, okay-dokey, and similar plums from the verbal wilderness of American good nature. He smiled amiably. He was reassuring. He was a good egg and let the world know he was a good egg. He was well groomed. He had been in the movies and emitted a modest whiff of celebrity, though not many people had ever seen a movie in which he acted. He was always in a "have a good day" mood. Although there already were a lot of termites in the dilapidated house of communism, he vowed to be the wrecking ball. He didn't worry. Like the newly rich, he spent money lavishly, in his case, the nation's money.

To those of us in rural Maine who were forking up our vegetable garden by hand and making our own tofu, furniture, cottage cheese, and quilts, among other things, it was strange and then some. A person whose existence was predicated on posing for cameras was considered extra-wholesome. We, who were committed to taking care of ourselves and sidestepping the blandishments of mass desire production, were marginal. How was that? What, we wondered, was wholesome to America? Perhaps an advertised smile. Perhaps the wealth that allowed people to live ultra-secure, segregated lives in gated communities. Perhaps a tired joke that everyone laughed at nonetheless. It didn't seem to be the bran muffins we were baking in the cook stove or the classic novels of childhood— *Black Beauty, Little Women,* or *Tom Sawyer*—we read to our children each night. Wholesomeness was one more image in the service of money. Linking wholesomeness with politics was a big leap of faith. The president's stature—what beyond smiling has this guy ever done—was unimportant. Indeed, it was reassuring. He seemed like a regular Joe, yet he was also a prince of some sort, an American, movie-world prince. In a republic where celebrity stands for aristocracy, someone who acts like a good-natured prince is a good-natured prince. Hollywood is the natural context for our myths to come true. Why shouldn't one walk off the movie lot and into the world at large? It seems unlikely that the United States has seen its last political prince.

Our need to believe is huge; the ugliness of ironic reality is irrelevant until such time as it overwhelms us. We briefly recognize it—arming the anti-Sandinista forces with money obtained by drug running during the "just say no" to drugs presidency—and then it subsides and another belief engulfs us. In pondering the nightmare of nationalist history, it is hard not to feel that nations lurch from mania to mania—ethnic and religious hatred, xenophobia, racism, colonialism, militarism—until their cumulative effect or one apocalyptic mania such as Nazism obviates that particular society. Too often, one horror replaces another.

While we pursued our Back-to-the-Land notions and I bartered poetry books for jars of homemade jam or maple syrup, the Reagan era moved imperturbably ahead by promoting the morality of greed. The United States has famously been about opportunity, which translates most readily into making money; what Reagan offered was good-natured mockery of idealism—to say nothing of social responsibility. Kennedy urged young people to serve their country. Reagan had no such urgings. He had made his money and believed that was what a person was here to do. If such individualism was concocted largely from selfishness and chose to demonize the public governmental arena as unnecessary and invasive, that was its moneyed right. He blessed the nation because the nation provided him with opportunity—a freedom more substantive than the rigmarole in the Bill of Rights. If you were a true-blue American, you didn't need those nonconformist rights such as protesting in public anyhow. Like a healer, the president's touch was precious. You might become him—tastefully glamorous, always in a good humor, and living the comfortable life.

We stared at ever-smiling newspaper photos of what seemed the apogee of thoughtlessness while sorting out carrot seeds to plant in the garden or listening to Glenn Gould play Bach on the boom box we had hooked up to a car battery. The counter-culture of which we were obvious representatives hadn't died, but it certainly seemed in exile. It hadn't taken America long to jettison us as a topic of interest and move on to yuppies. Yet, however laughably on the fringe we may have seemed, our bounded-by-the-woods prospect still seemed central. We were speaking to the earth and for the earth. We were building a small but genuine amount of soil. In our modest, composting, wood-burning way, we were doing what Gary Snyder once called the "real work." Much of what the nation at large was doing seemed unreal work—the proliferation of unnecessary necessities, sheer mischief.

Meanwhile, our president was a demigod of the sky. Satellites would keep away nuclear attacks. We barely needed the earth anymore. We could make endless money and spend endless money and not worry. We were the chosen people, but we didn't have to go and be missionaries anymore in places like China and Africa and get unpronounceable diseases. We could wave to the world from the heaven of our television. That, too, was a sky, a place of fantasy where no one really lived, a place without beginnings and endings.

What happens when a nation of small farmers no longer has contact with the earth? What happens when every human function is turned over to the genius of the profit motive? According to Ronald Reagan, nothing happened beyond some scurrilous poor people (probably of African American descent) trying to freeload while driving around in a Cadillac they didn't deserve. There were no consequences. This seemed to us, as we hauled one bucketful of water from the well after another, to be lunatic. If it didn't rain, your well went dry. But money, according to the Reagan creed, could do anything. Money could make there be enough water to irrigate endless lands and build endless cities in the desert. There was no stopping the power of money. Not even the primal weirdness of people smoking Mother Nature and lying back and staring for who knows how long at the clouds could stop money. They would have to get up. There were laws and ever more jails. Busy, domineering money had no use for unlicensed pleasures. Alcohol brought the retribution of a hangover; marijuana wore itself out in lassitude. It was good the president didn't hear those miscreants on the school bus. He might have had to frown.

We wanted our children to grow up wholesome, which meant to us that they would be people who savored their being on the earth and who took their responsibilities to others and to the earth seriously. Yet the president assured the nation it could do whatever it wanted and still be wholesome. He was. Just look at him. Did you ever see someone so genial and wholesome? Americans could buy more of what they didn't need and eat more of what didn't nourish them and never think twice about anything. Was it too good to be true? It had worked for him; he was a hero to many people. Meanwhile, our personal autarky continued along its quirky, muddy path. Sandwiches of tofu salad and clover sprouts were not being served at the White House.

My favorite task was splitting wood. Felling trees always felt dicey. In theory it was simple: you cut out a wedge on one side as close as was practicable to the ground (so as not to leave a high stump) and then cut into the other side to a point where you could insert a hardwood wedge. By driving the wedge further into the cut with the back of an axe head you could tip the tree over. In essence you were making a hinge. The tree fell because you had strategically weakened it. I was reasonably sure where the tree would fall, but a gust of wind might come along, or my cut might be off, or the tree might hang up on another tree. When with a powerful thud a fifty- or sixty-foot tree landed right where I wanted it to land, I breathed out deeply. Felling trees never was mundane; it was buzzing adrenaline. One way or another, something would give. When it gave properly, I was thankful. When something went amiss, I persevered. I couldn't walk away from a poorly cut tree. If I found myself cutting down a hung-up tree in two-foot sections until I had cut enough literally to wrestle it down, then I did that. It had to come down.

Cutting the fallen tree into lengths was a matter of vigilance. If the tree was lying on the ground, nothing dulled your chain as fast as cutting dirt. It was easy, too, to pinch the bar and have a stuck chainsaw. Sometimes I could drive a wooden wedge in the cut to create space for the chainsaw to loosen up. Other times I used an old-fashioned bow saw; I made cuts at an angle to the chainsaw and worked it out bit by bit. After I had cut the tree into four-foot lengths, I would lug the wood to a pick-up point, where I could load it onto whatever conveyance I was using that year. Even though a pulp hook gave you purchase on a log, you still were dealing with substantial amounts of unobliging weight. Tossing logs around, you understood why there were so many chiropractors in rural Maine.

Splitting wood was an acute mix of art and science. I used a splitting maul and a metal wedge. The maul had a long handle and a heavy head that was more compact yet more massive than an axe head. The bladed front of the head was beveled to enter the wood far enough so that the head's force could split it or at least make a healthy indentation where the wedge would go. Some logs were two-feet long; they fit into the Jøtul, which was the main heating source for our house. Some were eighteen inches and fit into the small, Irish box stove in the children's ell that we lit at night to warm their rooms. Some were less than a foot. They went into the cook stove in the kitchen. Except for the very tips of limbs, I used the whole tree. I cut those tips into small pieces so they would go back into the earth sooner. In the midst of my work in the woods, I often took time to stare at the duff and the miracle of dissolution. It was slow, beautiful magic: everything—leaves, needles, trees, plants, corpses—became the precious crumble of soil. As fascinations went, it was one I kept to myself; I realized that rot didn't do much for most people.

Despite the brute strength involved and metal clangor, splitting wood was meditative. You looked at each piece and sized it up as to where you would first strike. If, for instance, there were knots—where a limb had grown—you worked around them rather than trying to split right through them. If you tried to split through knots, your maul would bounce back. The wood was so tight, so gnarled, that the blade could not enter. Some trees were so large ("bears" to use Caleb's word) that, even if I could drive a wedge through the center, I still might not split the round in half. Instead, the wedge would embed itself. Sometimes I had to resort to the chain saw to rescue a stuck wedge. I learned to chip off sections around the circumference and so diminish the overall size. It took patience but saved grief, a lesson I kept learning.

Watching the riven pieces fall was a pragmatic and predictable pleasure, as was watching the pile grow over an hour or two. Eventually I carried those split pieces to one of the pole woodsheds I had built, where the wood would dry and be used in due time. At both ends of a row, I laid the split logs in layers that were perpendicular to one another. They formed pillars that supported the wood in-between. We never had much money in the bank, but we had wood in the shed. This was the old-time, Yankee way of life—stove wood in the shed and canned goods in the cellar. We would be warm; we had the basis for our meals; the hopeless world at large could do whatever it did. I came to understand how the industrious farmers of yore looked down on the improvident souls who, according to folklore, started burning chairs in March when the weather was still cold and the woodpile depleted. Stanton was usually three years ahead on his wood.

The area where I split wood was, in the local parlance, a wood yard. Whole, felled trees were waiting to be cut up, along with various lengths of limbs and sections of trunks. I had a stout round of maple upon which I split whatever log I was dealing with. The sounds that went with splitting wood were distinctive. There was the thick whack of the initial blow to the wood. Then, if I was using the metal wedge, came the precise, initial tap to set the wedge into the incision. Then there was the downward strike of the back of the maul head on the wedge. It was a ringing, brutal sound—one piece of metal meeting another. Almost simultaneously the wood would speak—a sound that varied from a strong "kerthunk," to a distinct tearing, to a sort of loosening sigh as the two pieces came apart. Sometimes both pieces fell apart cleanly. Other times a piece might wobble in a little awkward dance before falling. Other times both stood straight up. Every strike of the maul created a bit of gestural theater; within the precincts of the task were endless variations. Every sort of wood—ash, red maple, beech, gray birch, white birch, aspen—split somewhat differently. According to its size and grain and knots, every piece of wood was unique. I found enchanting the task that Caleb had worn out as a boyhood chore and that he coun-seled me to relegate to a gas-powered, hydraulic splitter. He shook his head with mock disgust when he saw me sweating at my end-less work.

I loved the splitting for its balance of the mindful and the mind-less. You studied the log and the grain of the wood; then you went to work. When you aimed the blade of the axe or maul, you couldn't will it. Your whole body—feet planted, legs bent forward a bit at the knee, back arched, arms taut but loose enough to bring the maul down—was engaged. Your eyes scrutinized the top of the log for its center; your hands brought the blade that was attached to the end of the handle to that place. Over the years, as might be expected, my aim improved. I didn't just see the wood; when the maul's blade hit it directly in its center, I was, in a sense that beggared language, right there with it. I never read the book about Zen and archery because it already made sense to me. Splitting wood was my ar-chery. Despite the work's roughness, it possessed that collaborative elegance of eye and hand that is distinctively human.

Hayden Carruth has remarked that manual labor is salutary for a writer. It's when your body and your practical mind—watch out for that knot, one swing more will do it—take over. Even on a good writing day there is an undercurrent of strain. You are trying to get every word right, but every word doesn't want to be right. You are bound to walk into any number of false oases. The woodpile ab-solved me of words. How many times did I experience a phrase jumping into my head when I was occupied with wood splitting? In forgetting the poem on my pad, my subconscious remembered. It happened over and over. I learned to trust that my imagining wasn't something that occurred specifically when I sat down with a piece of paper. I was the medium, not the controller. I wasn't trying to find anything; I didn't have to worry. The hard, at times fierce work with wood eased me. One subterranean way or another, the words came. That seemed how poetry should occur. You allowed for its presence; it had its own motions.

❧

The Road Washes Out in Spring

W hen I pulled from a self-addressed stamped envelope a little slip that stated a journal could not "use" my poems, I reflexively considered the wages of my curious calling. Most days I felt frustration about my work not being perceived for its merit (a stubborn authorial prejudice). Other days I felt confusion about whether I had sent the right poems to the right journal, dismay about opening myself again to rejection from complete strangers, or simple humility—I needed to look more closely at the poems to see how I could make them better. Revision took months and years; I had to stay with it. Eventually I would hit the wall of finitude, but one mercy of the endeavor was that it took time.

Common to almost every self-evaluation that a "we-can't-use-these" slip brought on was a tremor of alienation. The weirdness of the endeavor—writing poems that were sent to people I would never meet in the hope of receiving some validation that I was, indeed, writing poems—would hit me like a load of *trompe l'oeil* bricks. I, the putative poet, was in classic American fashion "expressing myself," expelling the spirit juice inside me and literally putting myself out there. So were untold thousands of others. Together—though we did not exist together in any physical form— we constituted a sort of congress of poetic egos. "Listen to me," each of us piped up in those personal narratives and lyrics that dominated the era. When I once asked a friend who worked as an editor at a poetry journal what it was like looking at thousands of those poems, she replied in a voice that contained more than a tinge of sarcasm, "An endless wave of self."

From what I knew of poetry's origins and development on this earth, it seemed more a tribal art than a self-ish one. A person learned a hoard of words and told the tribe's stories. Or a person had a vision and communicated that. Or a person was apprenticed to learn the lore of the tribe and how it must be passed on. Or a person memorialized whatever tragedies and victories occurred to the tribe. Whatever was being imparted, poetry depended on rhythm, sound, and memory to instill itself. The poet was a bard whose forms and subjects insisted on their intensity. The individual was folded into the embrace of something larger and deeper, something profound in the root sense of the word—profound as in "at the bottom." The afflatus that the word "poetry" still retains, its residual magic, must lie in this feeling of shared spirit work. The world of seers, mages, shamans, witches, prophets, wizards, and charmers was a crucial dimension of what poetry was. The dream of reason was, as far as poetry was concerned, exactly that—a dream. Existence was and is imaginative. Such is the shifting, perpetual, fantastic ground upon which poetry stands.

What such roots had to do with a nation of mass individuals, many of whom subscribe to the reductive, explanatory insights of psychology, was very sketchy. In some sense the political nation at large constituted a tribe, as in Whitman's poetry, though it was hardly a unified tribe. Walt proclaimed himself to be an American bard with an accompanying barrow load of American hokum, but he was the real, vatic thing. He possessed a vision, at once encompassing and microscopic. He entered other souls, and others—many others—entered his soul. He believed in the powers of democracy and poetry as they testified to the funky but noble scent of each and every life—beginning with his own. His organic, sprawling, testifying Self generated empathy, not narrowness. On a smaller but very vivid scale in the nation, there could be spontaneous tribes such as the Beats who proclaimed a vision ("I saw . . .") or the Harlem Renaissance movement to which others gravitated. Mostly, however, everyone was on his or her own to make art, the status of which in the society at large was very uncertain.

In this sense, Emily Dickinson seems as crucial an American poet as Whitman, the poetically appropriate counterweight. She wrote for herself and for a world beyond her that also was within her. In her proud, gnomic fashion she was a female shaman as she wrote taut, vital spells that queried and cast out the bleak, loveless religion in which she was brought up. She was doing work that needed to be done to the American psyche, although no one at the time knew it; most men and women who spoke for poetry were lost in the polite wastelands of gentility. Dickinson's narrator confronts puzzlement and indifference; the poems are both ordeals and initiations. In the sublime, quirky, defiant leaps of her lines, the habit of inwardness that the Puritans raised up and subjugated found its most original exemplar. Dull certainty and complacency are always staring her in the face; so is delight. Existence is both sweetly plain and darkly mortal. The poet perseveres. That the poet is a woman who honed her wit on neglect matters hugely.

Whitman wanted to please but didn't. Dickinson didn't want to please and would have laughed at the notion. She pleased herself (as did Whitman), and that had to come first. There is no poetry without the thrill (however arduous) of writing the poem. In the sense of the poet experiencing the magic of language, that thrill is sufficient. Yet poetry remains social in the tribal sense. It wants to get out there in some fashion. It wants its illuminations to enter other souls. It wants the embodiment of spirit that is poetry to be acknowledged.

The modern answers to the dilemma are understandable but dubious. Ezra Pound is thus a great poet in a handful of poems and as great a publicist, someone who articulated a vision of poetry's centrality and never let go, though to his lasting detriment. He was a combatant, an agonist, who set the stage for the self-consciously modern poet—someone who takes the weight upon him or herself. The unhappy irony is that the harried, self-absorbed society is not asking the poet to take on that weight. One finds in the lives of the mid-twentieth-century poets, in particular, a crisis where the disjunction between the intensity of the poet and the indifference and narrowness of the society is too great. Almost literally the poet implodes.

The answer was to make the best of the inglorious situation, precisely what occurred in the latter half of the twentieth century in the United States. Poets got busy creating programs, workshops, courses, degrees, prizes, publications, conferences, and other paraphernalia of a knowledge-oriented, mass society. Various tiny tribes grew up accordingly, with their various bards. If the center no longer held, there was an exciting amount of energy whirling around on the periphery. Perhaps it was a Great Periphery, as on those medieval maps that named legendary places like the Land of Prester John.

The position of the bard is a vulnerable one. The bard must tell the society both what it wants to hear and what it needs to hear. That the latter may not be what the society desires goes without saying. The poet's medium gives pleasure as it weaves sounds and rhythms, but the poet is not an entertainer in the sense of someone who agreeably makes time pass. Vision is the poet's key, but vision can take the poet places that may not be pleasing. On the contrary, they may be distinctly unsettling. Though the poet's work is rooted in praise as it traffics in the benign hoard of existence (the myriad things that elicit the myriad words), there is much the poet touches on that is malign. Neither Medusa nor Grendel nor the Inferno is an amiable vision.

This fact makes it all the more tempting for the poet to want to please. The poet wishes to be applauded, but to be liked, not infrequently, is to be compromised, to tell people at some artistic cost what they want to hear and thus become the poet who proffers sentimentality, relentless affability, surefire epiphanies, nonstop jokes, and various other quips and capers. To uphold poetry by diminishing it is a sad spectacle. The other tack—making the audience feel it is stupid—is no better. Cleverness is a poor substitute for soul. Given the difficult situation (for, because it seeks to wring beauty out of language that is sculpting time, poetry is a very daunting endeavor), it seems best to recognize the perils and to acknowledge that poetry is a primal search that asks the imperative, coaxing question, "What is that?" For poetry the question never goes away; poetry is rooted in wonder and never grows up. War, a broken affair, a piece of cake left on a plate, a bird that swoops by and disappears are all on the same plane of interrogation, questing, and feeling. Whether the envelopes pulled out of the mailbox on the backwoods, dirt road in Maine from the *Whatever Review* signal rejection or acceptance, the challenge to discover a living, visionary force remains. There always is Walt to hearken to: "I have perceived that to be with those I like is enough . . ."

<hr />

One October morning I received a call from the principal of the high school in which I worked. His voice had a high, choked quality as if he were gasping for air. "The library is on fire, Baron," he wheezed. For a second, I thought he meant the library in our little town. If a fire were to start there, the wooden structure would go up in flames in minutes. He couldn't mean the high school, which was a massive, impregnable-looking, 1920s brick building, a fortress that generations had attended, but he did.

When, after an unreal car ride in which I tried to tell myself this was a dream, I arrived, I saw a dense cloud of gray and black smoke above the .school. Yellow-red flames were shooting out the windows. I had never seen such a large building on fire. I thought of Dresden in World War II, of entire blocks with such buildings on fire, and how unbelievable the heat must have been. Someone told me the chemistry lab on the second floor had blown up. There had been a great jet and whoosh of flame. The whole two-story building was on fire, and that meant that the library, around ten thousand books, most of which I had selected one by one over the course of fourteen years, was destroyed. I stood there as if hypnotized.

Onlookers had to stand on the sidewalk across Main Street because the fire was so intense. The local fire departments were shooting water, positioning hoses, barking into walky-talkies. Police were rerouting traffic. On the front lawn lay a wooden dictionary stand for the unabridged dictionary that had stood on top of the library's card catalogue. The heat had blown out the school's windows and this one object with it. Later I retrieved it. It was singed in places but still intact. I wasn't sure what sort of memento I was being presented with.

No reflection on transience affected me quite the way those burning books affected me. Photos of Nazis feeding a bonfire with books and raising their arms in jubilation made me heartsick. It was one thing to talk about the downfall of civilization; it was another to burn books. I believed in books as an article of faith. How many afternoons had I gone to the local branch of the Enoch Pratt Free Library in my hometown of Baltimore and borne a stack of books home with me? I had read my way through modest swathes of that library—classic American and British fiction, poetry, world history, philosophy. Books were precious, and their keeping was precious. No one could ever sum up the work that had gone into their making. I tried to impress upon my students that real people had written the books and that they, too, could grow up to write books. It was—right down to the Harlequin romances and horror stories—a noble profession. Writers honored language, and language was worth honoring. To burn a book was an impiety.

The school was a small high school in a mill town that was less than a bastion of education. Still, the books had their own lives and were indifferent to reputation. Hands and minds that were ardent, curious, or merely dutiful had handled them. Always mute, they spoke nonetheless. They had been borrowed and returned or occasionally stolen (rock and roll, automotive manuals, and sexual information were at the top of the most-purloined list) and taken elsewhere to reside. Or they simply sat there waiting. The waiting was part of their lives, and they didn't mind it. Libraries were about patience, possibility, and persistence. Libraries were an ode to longevity. The chief fact was that each book existed. Now they didn't. The dense, bitter smoke made my stomach turn. I watched the long hoses pour water through the empty windows into the blackened stacks.

People must have tried to console me, but I don't remember hearing anyone. I stood there and stared for what seemed like a long time. In all likelihood it was only a few minutes. The principal gathered us to meet in a nearby hall to assess what had happened and what we would do. Again, I don't remember much of that. My mind was fumbling with something it had never encountered. I knew about personal loss from my mother's death, but this was another kind of loss. I had lost years of caring and attentiveness to the blank rage of destruction. I was staring at a sort of finality and elemental emptiness that left me dazed. I had assumed the books—flimsy as they were—were something like forever. Paper yellowed and grew brittle, but that took a long time. How sheltered I had been to think I was somehow beyond the reach of a spark or a match.

Like most people at the scene I assumed the fire was the outcome of a spark. It was an old building; bad wiring was blamed for many fires. That must have been what happened to us. The state fire marshal came and started to sift through the debris. Meanwhile, we found ourselves in another school across the Kennebec River that hospitably allowed us to use their facility so our students could continue their education. In the late afternoon of our first day in the building, while trying to figure out where things were in a library I had never been in before, our janitor, Ray, came in and asked me if I smelled anything funny in the air. I sniffed and said that I did. Very slowly we walked down the hallway outside the library; like two hounds we kept sniffing. The halls were empty; everyone was in classes. Outside the boys' room, Ray stopped. The smell seemed to intensify there. He told me to wait and keep an eye out. He fetched a stepladder, then went in and popped a few tiles from the hung ceiling. A gallon can of gasoline and a few old hand towels were perched on an intersection of the ceiling supports. He came out and shook his head. "We've got some real trouble," he said.

Within minutes state troopers descended on us. At a hasty, after-school meeting, the principal, who thankfully was an even-tempered person, told us not to panic. We should not jump to conclusions. In any case, we were not going to be pushed around by some pyromaniac kid. He did not say "pyromaniac kid," actually. Like Ray, he, too, shook his head when telling us about the gasoline can and the towels. His voice was trying to stay calm, but it had the quaver in it of the morning of the fire, a this-can't-be-happening voice. That pyromaniac kid was in all likelihood one of our students. We were looking at him every day. We were teaching him. He was watching us. And God knows what was going on in his head. I thought that Stephen King did not live and write in our state for nothing. We might be poor and rural, but we had our share of craziness. That awful momentum when a human mind goes off the tracks and doesn't look back was palpable. That awful vortex of obsessive destruction was imaginable.

I found myself scrutinizing students. Could the sophomore girl who was idly looking at an article in *People Magazine* about worst-dressed people break into a building, douse the thick auditorium curtains with gasoline, strike a match, and stand there smiling with pleasure as the flames started up? She looked like a good kid who had other things to do than burn down schools. Maybe it was the guy next to her who was trying to impress her with the car he was going to buy. Maybe she wasn't impressed, and he needed to do something really impressive. Or maybe it was a kid who never came into the library because he hated books; he had been in a remedial reading group and would just as soon schools did not exist and had decided to do something about it. Or it was a loner who had read some of Stephen King's novels and thought it was time for her to try out some scariness for herself. Or it was a model kid who was helping to carry the dozens of boxes of books people donated into the library where I could cull them. I looked at an open box and spied yet another copy of James Michener's *Hawaii*. I could have used a vacation there. Suspicion was a miserable thing.

A few weeks later I walked into work to learn that overnight someone had tossed a Molotov cocktail through a window of the junior high school that stood beside the black shell of the high school. It had not caught; the school had not burnt down. After that incident, to say that people felt under siege would have been an understatement. In a small town, everyone knows everyone, a closeness that gets under your skin in peculiar ways. People rely on one another; almost everyone in his or her way has a role in the community. Now there was someone who had the role of public terrorist. People talked about moving in with kin in other towns. Rifles were ready to shoot something besides a deer.

Naturally, there was much animated conjecture as to who this person might be. Sneaker tracks had been found in the snow outside the junior high. "It probably ain't no grandmother doin' this," a local at the restaurant across from the paper mill opined one morning to anyone who cared to listen. The *New York Times* sent up a stringer from Boston to do a story. He talked to workers coming off their shift at the mill. One told him that it must be some kid; he would know what to do with that kid. Kids weren't disciplined enough nowadays. The article had to make anyone glad that he or she didn't live in some weird mill town in the middle of Maine. Maybe the whole, woebegone, squirrelly place would go up in smoke.

Our student, a sophomore boy who was in the college division, played in the band, and was very polite in school, did try to send the whole place up in smoke. One night he threw some Molotov cocktails into people's houses. People were in the houses at the time. He was apprehended relatively quickly. Later it came out that he had been setting grass fires since he was a boy. This had been considered by the police a nuisance but tolerable. Boys would be boys.

Jamie was remanded to the youth center; not long afterward, his family moved away. He would no longer bring in cartons of donated books to me and cheerfully ask me where I would like him to set them down. He would no longer stand around joking with other guys about matches. He would no longer tell me in a voice that was trying to be serious how sad all this was and that, upon reflection, I thought contained more than a hint of mockery. In one of those fits of cosmic irony the universe is so big on, his father had been the guy who told the *Times* that he would know how to handle such a kid. The wheels of psychology began to churn out explanations for our student's behavior. I listened, but those wheels didn't bring back my charred library.

Having endured fire, I then faced water. In the spring of that year, the Kennebec River experienced a catastrophic, hundred-year flood. The thousands of books I was collecting to start a new library were stored in an old mill directly beside the Kennebec. When I called the superintendent of schools' office to ask what shape the building was in, a secretary told me it could only be reached by boat. I put down the phone and sighed a long sigh. It turned out that mill employees kept pumps going, and the water never reached the floor the books were on. Days later I walked in and smelled the funky dampness and silt the river had deposited in the building's basement. My notions of what should and shouldn't happen dissolved into thankfulness for what was. I picked up a random book from the makeshift shelves and began reading. Any words would do.

❧

Our family's big night out consisted of a trip to the movies in Waterville. I think of this as happening in winter because immediately I remember the children going through the labors of putting on their jackets, boots, hats, and mittens and walking out of the house in the late afternoon darkness. I would stoke the stove, leaving the draft wheel on its front door open a dite (one of my favorite Maine words) to keep the fire going. I would check that there was plenty of wood in the wood box for when we returned. Janet would peer into the cast-iron kettle on top of the stove to make sure water was in it. The air got very dry in a wood-heated house; the kettle gave off a modest amount of vapor. One of us would let out the two dogs (some combination of Webster, Buffy, Fritzi, or August, in the order of their appearances in our lives) and call them back in. Sometimes we would remember to bring a flashlight with us for when we returned to the house, sometimes not. Despite our routine diligence, Janet and I often were too distracted by whatever it was we were talking about at the moment—artistic, political, historical, or personal—to be purely methodical. The four of us finally piled into the Subaru to drive the twenty-some miles past dark houses, houses lit by the marvel of electric light, and endless snow-spangled trees.

Our destination was the Railroad Square Cinema, an alternative movie house started in the 1970s by newcomers to Maine. The Square was a cultural mecca for those who had come of age amid the *auteur* excitement of the 1960s and then found themselves living in the cinematic wilds of central Maine. The small towns had charming, old-time theaters in brick buildings that showed one box office smash each weekend. The large towns had unlovely, big box buildings that contained four or five theaters that also showed "boffo" (to quote *Variety*) movies. Anything less than a mega-Hollywood-star movie was off the map. For those of us who had become devotees of Truffaut, Antonioni, and Godard, who had stood in line to see *Easy Rider,* and who had argued in our heads with Andrew Sarris and Pauline Kael, the pabulum of mayhem, cleavage, and spaceships didn't cut it.

The Square was lodged in an old warehouse space near the railroad tracks. It consisted of a small theater with passable though hardly comfortable seats and an attached restaurant where we dined on vegetarian chili, lentil soup, and salads topped with sprouts, sunflower seeds, and yogurt dressing—the age of the *Moosewood Cookbook*. The restaurant and cinema were counter-cultural hangouts; walking into them on a frigid, bleak, winter evening felt like entering a clubhouse. Most people were bundled up in the colorful woolen wear that hippies favored—ski caps, sweaters, and scarves from around the planet or knit at home from local wool. There was a down-home aroma of wet boots, bodies that may not have showered recently, greasy popcorn, and coffee. I found the smell pleasing, but then I agreed with Walt Whitman in his praise of armpits. A fair number of these people were also carving out homesteads in the middle of Elsewhere. Our family wasn't alone in the endeavor. These people liked off-to-the-side movies, too.

I sometimes saw films that my sister, who at the time lived in New York City, didn't catch. The people who ran the Square and the people who tacked up suggestions on scraps of paper to a bulletin board were alert. It seemed like decades before John Sayles's movies made their way into the "big" theaters; our children grew up watching every movie that he made. (He was, along with Bob Dylan and Bob Marley, one of our family's cultural heroes.) Although going back and mining the titles—*Down by Law* or *My Life as a Dog* or *Desert Bloom*—would be an intriguing exercise in cinematic history, it was more the sense of the endeavor—on our part and on the filmmakers' part—that mattered so much. In a way, we were presenting the world to our children. It wasn't the televised, commercial, formulaic world. It was the world of what has come to be called "independent" movies—made by people who created the space to follow where their intuitions took them, using the chief art form of the twentieth century. I know from friends that more than one of the children sitting there with their earnest, Back-to-the-Land parents grew up to become involved in moviemaking themselves. It doesn't surprise me.

After the ninety-eight minutes were over, we bundled up again, trying to remember our scarves, hats, and gloves, and stumbled out into the cold. The ride home was sometimes animated with discussion and surmise or dreamy with each person lost in thought about whatever world the movie had conjured up. Most of the houses we drove by were dark now. Above us the winter sky glittered ruthlessly. We were another human family generating our own imaginative heat—some of it acute, and some of it confused. The world outside the car windows was desolate. Though we were likely to have said "hi" to someone we knew in the lobby of the theater and made some quick conversation, the evening had largely been devoted to communing with a vision that came from far away. We weren't local. It was hard to imagine we ever would be.

Part of living in the woods was listening to what the trees said. One thing they said was to endure. To see them so overhung with snow and ice that they seemed to be wearing great white overcoats, to hear them creak and shiver in the sub-zero cold and clatter in the northeast winds like so many paltry dice was to feel the lessons that their rooting and patient growth embodied. If you wanted to live, you wanted to persevere. When a tree did blow over, I looked carefully at the roots the wind had brought to light. A tree that was trying to grow where there was more granite than soil sent roots out in every direction to compensate for the taproot it could not form. It craved to be anchored. Its instinct for sustenance was cautionary. In the dull earth a drama was at work that the avid eye never saw. My noticing moments were random episodes. The earth was vast and infinitesimal; it beggared thought.

The trees said to be still. The Tao stressed that resistance to natural forces is futile. If our inner being is at peace, we bend but not break. When I spoke to people about poems, one quality I pointed out was the tremendous ability poems had to "dwell," to stay in the moment as long and as deeply as they could. The trees were remarkable dwellers; like monks, they lived in stillness. Each moment registered on them as they stood through the whirl of the seasons. They were sentient—the sap that flowed from a broken pine limb left a congealed scar and a long, tear-like track down the trunk—but sturdy. They were the stuff of breath and flow, yet they suspended themselves, too, drawing in through the long winter.

Their stillness conjured within me the longing for a similar stillness. Active as my life was—and daily I was splitting, sawing, or lugging wood, some days all three—I felt that I couldn't live indefinitely in the United States without a spiritual practice. Poetry, however affirming, was marginal in the society at large and subject to the unhappy temptation to consider reputation as an end in itself. I felt that poetry in many ways was a spiritual practice: one learned to work with one's shortcomings while trying to create something of value, one lived with and trusted spirit, one embraced the passion and precision of imagination. I felt, as I wrote poems about different people in different circumstances, that poetry was a pathway to empathy. Despite these feelings, I needed a deeper refuge on a day-by-day basis. There were too many holes in poetry; I didn't want to plug them with ego.

Meditation is paradoxical in that one sits still yet is engaged in a very strenuous activity: trying to acknowledge and let go of one's mental hubbub. Most of us accept that hubbub as life itself. The likes of Robert Lowell and John Berryman made great, anguished poetry from it. We build inside ourselves elaborate structures to accommodate that hubbub and run our lives accordingly. Yet for all my instinctive love of thinking, I found myself weary of the distracted parade of my thoughts—to say nothing of the hailstorm of others'. I knew that poetry existed in relation to silence, and I lived with that silence. At night in our house it was silent as the earth— no whirring motors, no cars passing by, no neighbors closing the garage door. I remained, however, full of internal noise, the typically human cacophony of anxiety.

Perhaps our house in the woods was a haven, but I needed a further haven, one that couldn't be seen and that conformed to no notions about anything. As I came to experience it, meditation, the mere sitting still, seemed the jewel the Buddhist sutras spoke of, an incomparable, unadvertised gift. For one wasn't trying. One was being. To the devouring, outward eye one was doing nothing. The unhappy dynamism of invention, of always making one thing into another seemed, in that small, simple act, to fall away. I didn't want anything from sitting. I simply wanted to do the sitting, to have that model in my life, that place where I could go and feel however imperfectly what I was—a breathing creature who someday would no longer be a breathing creature. I could feel my impermanence and be with it. I could feel the marvel of my breathing and attend to it. I could dwell with being alive as something unto itself rather than a route to other things.

Janet began sitting before I did, and so I joined her, bashfully at first, before a little altar she had created on a foot locker in our sleeping loft. The army-green trunk with its lock that no longer worked was a relic of her days at Girl Scout camp. On it sat a ceramic Buddha about six-inches high, two small memorial candles that we bought in the Woolworth's in Skowhegan, and an incense holder. The very notion of an altar intrigued and pleased me. Modest as it was, it represented something at once tangible and eternal to which we could orient ourselves. It felt integral to our house. It was another way station, a consecrated place within the place we had created. Like our house and the woods, it gave us the chance to feel who we might be.

Like many people of the Vietnam War generation, the photographs of the Buddhist monks who immolated themselves haunted me. What was this? I thought to myself. What were these people doing? They were people, weren't they? People who got up in the morning, ate a piece of fruit or a cracker, went into the street, patted an old dog, looked up at the sky, and thought, "This is beautiful, this sky." They had sat in a public space and set themselves on fire. I couldn't imagine a more powerful action to show the world—what? What did it show the world? Did it show the world how the flesh was easily consumed? Did it show the world that war accomplished nothing? Did it show the world how determined a human being could be? Did it show the world that we already lived in the fire of suffering, that identity was hell? Did it show that any certainty was a dim, passing illusion? I couldn't say exactly. Perhaps I would find a glimmer of accurate feeling for those monks. Perhaps I wouldn't feel that there was a chasm between them and me that couldn't be bridged. Perhaps I could learn to look into an abyss that wasn't an abyss.

Certainly I didn't meditate so that I could write a poem. Poems took care of themselves. Who knew what a Buddhist poem would look like? It might be life pared down to essentials—the unencumbered path where spirit could sing as the moment moved it. Then again, it might be a list that enacted the randomness of existence. It might be hushed; it might exclaim in a fiery, throaty voice. Buddhism sought to shake up the mind so that concepts fell away. The literary history I had studied and internalized was one, big, ongoing, conceptual barn dance. I felt how the tireless mind turned every nuance of expression into either/or shorthand—complex or simple, classical or romantic, avant-garde or traditional, politically laudable or politically retrograde. Dualism stretched into the sunset, a protean yet confining outlook. People sometimes asked me, "Are your poems happy or sad, because I don't want to read any sad poems that are going to depress me." I told them what poetry cared about was feeling. It didn't care about emotional distinctions. People would then look at me as though I was trying to fob off a Ford Pinto as a Mercedes. Get real, man, their eyes said. Who doesn't care about happy and sad?

One beautiful thing about meditating was that there was nothing to report about happy or sad, wise or unwise. One did it or didn't do it. There were no maps, gauges, or charts. Progress couldn't be determined in any supra-rational, inquisitive manner. I sat under the pine board eaves on a cushion and tried to be still. My mind told me that the dogs needed to be let out, that I was never going to get another book of poetry published, that I should have kissed Susan Katz on that first date in 1964, that I would die soon, that I didn't have enough money to make the next car payment. I didn't judge my thoughts. They were so many banners in the mental parade. I read that the ego was like the sole of a shoe; meditation wore the sole down. Sitting still was an action. The trees were alive. I was becoming a cousin to them. At the least I was trying. "Try, try, try—ten thousand years!" the Buddhists adjured. To the intent randomness of human actions and the scenarios that went with them, I was proposing stillness. For me, it made sense.

Although they were held throughout the summer, to me September seemed the proper time for a fair. September was the harvest month when we were busy canning tomatoes, making gazpacho and tabouli, and reveling in the fresh produce that we could cook with and that we lacked most of the year. Frost came in the form of a clear, windless night in late September or the beginning of October and wiped out all the delicate-leaved plants—the peppers, squashes, tomatoes, basil, eggplant. Sometimes we went out with blankets and sheets and covered them, because we couldn't bear to give them up. Or we watered the leaves early in the morning to try to take off the frost. Frost was fluky. Another week or two or even three of above-freezing temperatures might follow. Eventually, however, a hard frost in the mid-twenties would come; we would look out at blackened plants and resign ourselves to the inevitable. We threw the limp bodies onto the compost heap. The green glory of summer was gone.

Our favorite county fair was the Franklin County Fair held in the county seat (also known as the shire town) of Farmington, a two-traffic-light town with a population of seven thousand. It wasn't a big fair, but it wasn't so small that you self-consciously mourned the agricultural way of life that had been left behind. There were the usual scream-inducing rides, animal exhibits, booths that sold food, a few evening performances by third-tier country western singers, tractor and oxen pulls, and harness racing. Something for everyone, as the earnest, trying-to-be-excited voice on the local radio station touted it. The fair had begun well over a hundred years ago. Anything that went on in novelty-obsessed America for over a hundred years deserved some respect. Rural life waxed and waned, but the fairground with its creamy yellow, wooden exhibition halls, grandstand, animal sheds, pens, and stalls endured.

When our children were growing up, we didn't miss a year at the fair. Not much happened in our part of the world; the fair was a genuine spectacle. I still can feel the tingle in our children's little hands as we walked onto the fairground. They wanted to run off and do everything at once. At the same time, they wanted to stay close to us because they weren't used to seeing so many people in one place. A crowd was town meeting or a throng of moviegoers (though there rarely was a line of any sort). We stood there gawking, sniffing, and listening. One joy of the bustle was how it put your senses on overload. What smells like a cow, fried dough, diesel, cotton candy, and sweat? What sounds like a crying child, a bellowing steer, a shrieking teenage girl, a calliope (on tape, of course), and the bored yet avaricious come-on of a too-well-traveled carnie? It was all there, and all at once.

After the children had had their share of rides, we visited our favorite food concessions. These included Peter and Velma, the French Fry King and Queen, who traveled around New England towing their little white stand and methodically slicing and cooking up fifty-pound bags of spuds to crisp perfection. Our natural foods concerns about pure cooking oil vanished in the beckoning smell of those delectable fries. Then there were the various church groups that prided themselves on homemade pies and bean casseroles. During the rest of the year it was hard to get a decent piece of coconut cream pie in any local eatery, but not at the fair. At the fair you could choose between the Congregational ladies, the Baptist ladies, and the Methodist ladies. On account of their extra flaky crusts, we preferred the Baptists. For the finale there was make-your-teeth-fall-out fudge.

Full of delicious, bad food we wandered around and gazed. We looked over pigs, rabbits, cows, exotic fowl, chickens, horses, goats, and sheep. We talked about which kind of creature we might raise. In their straightforward, variously smelly animal presence, every species and type seemed endearing. They sniffed, they shifted a leg, they fluttered wings, they stared benignly ahead, they chewed, they whinnied, they snorted. Living as we did in the woods, the prospect of clearing sufficient land to make a place for animals was daunting. The responsibility of caring for them was daunting, too. But we felt a pang that—beyond our two dogs—we didn't have any animals. Taking care of animals seemed to us, as we walked up and down the rows of stalls, one of the most important things a person could do. Domesticated creatures had cast their lot with the human race. What were we to make of such trust? They stood between the romance of wildness and the brouhaha of the human head. No wonder Walt Whitman wanted to throw in his lot with them. We lingered and felt their natures entering ours. We, too, became ruminative until, with numerous backward glances, we left. Some situations don't resolve themselves. We knew we would be back again next year, sighing and delighting.

After the animals, we wandered around the exhibition hall. We pondered jars of string beans, enormous, strange-looking winter squash, gasoline-powered leaf shredders, flyers for local political candidates, purple cauliflower, yellow beets, gourds, crazy quilts, and itchy-looking afghans. Eventually we found ourselves before an open window and remembered the September night outside. The children were tired and more than ready to leave. As we walked to our car, I thought about how, when I was a boy, I never as much as saw a pea plant. Whatever I knew came from a can. Though I never voiced it to anyone, I had wanted to learn where the vegetables came from and grow them myself. There had to be more than those sad, grayish peas in their tasteless water. Whatever else the fair had become, it remained rural and tied to the ways of the earth. The succotash, penuche, and Tilt-a-Whirl made an improbable but soothing medley.

The other fair we went to was the fair started by people such as ourselves—the Back-to-the-Land types, the hippies from the Land of Away who wanted to do everything firsthand, who were in love with authenticity and hard work. It was the tofu fair, the organic fair, the goat's-milk-cheese fair, the grow-herbs-and-heal-yourself fair, the spin-your-own-wool fair, the support-your-local-seed-company fair. It was inspiring to feel how much let's-do-it energy was out there. On dirt roads throughout the state people were growing their own food, milling their own lumber, planting their own orchards, shearing their own sheep, and a plethora of similar, dirt-under-the-nails endeavors. To use an urban phrase, people were getting down.

It was as if everyone wanted to found a nation that would be a counter-nation to the unwieldy one we lived in. Everyone wanted to found a kingdom in the deep sense of the word, a world unto itself that was beneficent and whole, that didn't partake of the isolating fragmentation of modernity. This effort wasn't exciting in the sense that modern society valued media excitement. It was quiet, alert, and personal. These people wanted to learn everything they could about the old ways. The fair showed that the Back-to-the-Landers were learning and could teach others. The spontaneous movement of youngish people to the country was putting down roots. Although some became discouraged by the isolation and marginal economy and moved on, others stayed. They liked dying fabrics with native plants, building saunas and chicken coops, espaliering pear trees and pollinating heirloom plants. They liked bothering with what no one bothered with anymore.

There was no Tilt-a-Whirl at the Common Ground Fair (as it was known). There were games for children to participate in, but they were simple games such as tag or a sack race. The electro-corn-fed glow that a state fair had and that America instinctively loved wasn't what this fair was about. It wasn't a release from daily life into a world that throbbed with curiosities and scream-aloud thrills. It was more like treasured daily life writ large. It was a celebration of an economy of living, an economy that deserved to be celebrated. Perhaps because it didn't amount to anything money-wise and didn't have to deal with the pressures that regular farmers had to deal with, it could afford to be modest. Farmers had to cope with a world of banks, commodity markets, equipment manufacturers, wholesalers, and retailers that had no use for small farms—"get big or get out" was the curt adage. The landscape of pastures turning into building lots testified to that attitude. Compared to those determined souls who kept farms going through the decades, the people at the fair were novices. Yet they were serious novices who were finding their own way. "Life can go deeper" was one enticing theme that the 1960s sang. These people were living that song. Our family was living that song.

One year Wendell Berry came to the fair and talked. It was in a sort of agricultural hall. I seem to remember bales of hay lying around. That setting was appropriate, because what Berry was saying was what his audience believed—the land mattered, and how we treated the land mattered. You judged a culture by what it did with its land. If it mistreated its land, it was going to mistreat its children and its animals. It was going to forget where anything came from. It did not look forward to passing on the stewardship of the earth to another generation, because it sought only to extract what it could from the earth for the sake of profits. It was not a culture, because cultures grow values that are rooted in time-honored actualities, but an agglomeration of people following fads, trends, and random oc-currences—or not even that, merely so many competing individu-als, so many whirling, nightmarish atoms. It thrived on ignorance and indifference. In the background to its delirium, the great pulse of the earth kept beating.

I doubt that anyone in the hall that sunny, mild, autumn after-noon felt that everyone should be a farmer, gardener, or sheep raiser or that most people shouldn't live in cities. It was rather that the car-ing on which rural life was based deserved respect and merited at-tention. We couldn't legislate caring; we certainly couldn't buy it. It was human and needed the earth for it to happen. The path of the United States had been to use the earth, then forget it as if the vast-ness of the continent could absorb anything, as if the mental notion of endless frontiers was more substantial than the testimony of culti-vating one piece of ground. The ghosts of thousands of small farms testified that caring—however tenacious and deeply felt—didn't pay. Though everyone was in thrall one way or another to the cap-italized god known as The Economy, that didn't mean that people had to buy into it wholly. Simple living was an option.

We left the fair with a feeling of resolution. We were going to grow different varieties of summer squash next year or try out a solar panel or compost our outhouse shit or go help peasants in Cen-tral America. The fair incited us to dream ourselves further into our lives. It didn't promote a notion of the future where humans would let machines do their living for them. Rather it promoted the sense of humans locating themselves in the present moment of the ancient earth. When we returned to our house, we stared for some seconds at the September night sky. It was getting cool. Maybe we would start a fire when we got in to take the chill off. Maybe we would make a cup of tea. The children held our hands as we walked in the dark. There was, of course, no light in the yard. The crickets were sawing away, while inside the house our two dogs yipped in anticipation. I opened the unlocked door, groped my way to where the matches were, and struck one to light a kerosene lamp. I imagined the other people who had been at the fair entering their houses, turning on lights, and looking around at whatever they called "home."

We humans are domestic creatures who lay down at night and take meals each day yet live within the vastness of the cosmos. How hard it is to balance the small with the large, to not become obsessed with one at the expense of the other, to be neither narrow nor dwarfed. Many nights in all seasons I stood outside and tried to take the night in, not making it into something—not even into words—but letting it be. How could we ever give thanks enough? Beyond the prospects the fair kindled, it made us consider the occasions of thankfulness that always were present. If we chose to ignore them in our busy-ness, that was our loss. It seemed that peoples shouldn't be judged on the basis of what they did as much as what they revered. It could be the dirt beneath their feet.

※

In his "Birches," Robert Frost wrote of "Some boy too far from town to learn baseball, / Whose only play was what he found himself." Our children did learn baseball; they had each other to play with, but they did live far from town. In "The Hill Wife," Frost noted of the wife that "It was too lonely for her there." Frost had a powerful sense of how the country could be isolating, how solitude was a companion but only up to a point. Beyond that point lay fear and desolation, a feeling of being left behind or left out or not even being known to other people, of disappearing.

In an age devoted to psychological explanation and adjustment, that loves to measure itself against whatever norms science currently proposes and that seeks to justify itself by its adherence to those norms, the notion of going off and living apart in the woods seems at best whimsical, at worst downright destructive of whatever putative mental health one might have. Without getting into a discussion of the mythical domain of the "normal," it would be fair to say that ours was a way of living that was bound to create differences. As a family, for instance, we spent a great deal of time with each other. Our downstairs consisted of one, large, open room. The children had their bedrooms; we had a sleeping loft. That was it. There was no den, dining room, study, recreation room, or living room. This arrangement, of course, is not uncommon on much of the planet; as a relative of Janet's who visited us once exclaimed, "This is like the third world!" Our modest house with its spruce floors, tongue and groove pine walls, and double-hung windows was palatial compared to most of the world, but in terms of space, of the one room where everything occurred, she was right. In many of those third world villages, there were other family members around to help raise the children. Janet and I had no such nearby relatives. For the first twelve or so years of our children's lives, we never spent a night during which we were both away from them.

Accordingly, we hung out a lot. As I once wrote in a poem:

> At night they sit around the table
> And sketch, write letters, read,
> Complain, tell jokes, pick their teeth,
> Discuss life in terms of a fable

There was plenty of chance to get in one another's way, which we did at times. My tuneless singing could get on anybody's nerves. Yet the spirit of the enterprise was communicated to our children through our labor and through the cooking that went on day in, day out: we are a family, and a family lives together. Our being together stood in contradistinction to the semblance of companionship the television provides for Americans. My dad had given us a television before we moved to the woods, but we didn't want it and took it to the town dump. Later, I asked the dump attendant what happened to it. He said he used it, but one night Richard Nixon came on and he shot it.

There was plenty of music generated by the boom box we had hooked up to a car battery and that allowed us to play the radio and cassettes. Our kids grew up hearing a standard ton of rock and roll to say nothing of the reggae soundtrack of *The Harder They Come.* We danced, sang along, and spent many Saturday nights listening to the local Oldies show where the disk jockey reminisced in a friendly, nasal voice about his favorite Beatles' tunes. I listened to the Red Sox on the radio, particularly enjoying the descriptions of the long-time announcer, Ned Martin. A former English major, his words were measured, astute, and, at times, poetic; he quoted from Shakespeare and Hemingway. Since the Red Sox were a heartbreaking team, his talent for consoling metaphor was appreciated. The quiet remained, however, our basic companion. Though I knew that for many people silence brought uneasiness, for me it was deliverance. A red squirrel gathered pinecones or the clouds drifted by or a chickadee announced itself or I splintered the helve of an ax or the children ran up and down the driveway playing tag. Whatever occurred was life on earth as it occurred; we never turned to television to provide a distracting time-out.

From our rustic vantage point, an episode of a situation comedy, cartoon, or melodrama was just that; the particular episode reinforced a given notion. This guy was funny, this guy was pathetic, this guy was a slob. Like fast food, predictability was comforting. As to the news that television purveyed, its glossy, assertive presentation buried any pretense at thought. There were wars and car crashes, there was going to be weather tomorrow, athletes made lots of money, movie stars got divorced. Everything was grist for the glad glow of oblivion. For us there was no glow. Television wasn't exciting; it was a rumor of life. When our children grew up and rehearsed their various complaints about their childhood in the woods—the lack of playmates, our being tied down to the house, the embarrassment of living differently, the claustrophobia of the experience, their absorbing more of our personalities than they ever wanted—they never cited the absence of television. Their indifference to growing up without television wasn't about virtue on anyone's part and how inevitably it was better to read a book. It was that a diet of television took away our time to be human, that it sucked out our reflective inwardness. As the wall of novels in the school library indicated, our being human was problematic, but it was who we were and preferable to staring at a magic world that purveyed not so much magic as the ability to make time pass agreeably. What sort of time was that?

There was plenty of room in that little house to doubt ourselves, and we did. After getting down from an ice hacking session on the roof or pondering whether the road was passable because of snow, rain, or mud or getting diarrhea on a January night, we had to wonder what we were doing and where we were doing it. In a world that was more and more obsessed with trying to minutely control experience—right down to every moment of a child's day or every mouthful a person took in—we were pursuing a sense of life that nestled in the depth and sprawl of timelessness. When we watched the snow descending ever so gently on the boughs of the conifers that stood on all sides of the house, or when on a June morning we marveled at the prisms of dew on the vetch and daisies and the spider webs in Ella and Stanton's field, however, the isolation fell away. We were connected in more ways than we ever could count. There was no sum, just infinite entries.

The questions about what we were doing and why we were doing it did not go away. A friend in a neighboring town used to tell inquisitive people, "They live under a big tree in a big, cozy hole." He'd smile goofily and wave his arms like a swami to show how mystifying it was. "They eat bushels of acorns and sleep on mattresses stuffed with corn husks." The curiosity was understandable enough. What was hard to explain in a land of buying, selling, and accumulating was how wealth could be irrelevant. Simplifying was an old story but tended to get forgotten. It wasn't dynamic; it didn't make anything important happen. Its promises lacked glamour.

What Robert Frost felt in his rueful, astute, impassioned way was how living with the earth was the most engaging experience there was. It was the eternal drama and the primal scene; all social notions were so much persiflage. It was the bottomless, variegated miracle that didn't care a lick if you paid attention or not. It was the draft of time you never could drain, the immensity you never could circumnavigate. A passion for the earth severed you from the nodding complacency that passed for knowledge. You were likely to pay a price for such a way of living, a price it would be dishonest to minimize. The day our children got on the school bus, they were called out, subtly and not subtly, for being different. Although clearly a pre-eminent talent, Frost was scorned by more than one progressive as a coy hick and hopeless reactionary.

From the perspective of a largely urban society, the countryside was a memento of an ancient feeling. It was suitable for framing as a pastoral keepsake, for pickling in nostalgia, or for subdividing for profit, but it was essentially done with. The city had won. When, however, we got down on our hands and knees in the field across the road and picked tiny, wild strawberries as sweat trickled down our faces, or we scuffed maple leaves on a late October afternoon or lay down at night with the darkness or a thousand other physical occasions, we felt ourselves held in the spell of something we needed desperately. I think that a sort of desperation, a longing that cared nothing for fluent reasons, was why we lived the way we did for so long. Accepting the earth's beauty and our own intensity took time. Only in shared solitude could that happen.

✻

Our family's years together in the woods were knit together by numerous rituals. With each season there arrived "firsts": the first asparagus from the asparagus patch, blueberries from the high bush blueberry plants, snowflake, yellow warbler, lady slipper, or jack-in-the-pulpit. Our acknowledgment was an exclamation rather than a ceremony, but the exclamation stood in the context of time and conjured a stirring sense of the returning flower or bird. There were cooking rituals—making dill pickles each August, clafouti (a delectable berry dessert), or plum torte with plums from the plum tree we had planted, or canning tomatoes and ketchup and green tomato chutney. Implements we didn't use throughout the rest of the year were dusted off dutifully. Each year I stared at the dark stains in the maple bowl in which I made the basil sauce called "pesto." I sniffed the scarred bowl and could smell other summers. I ran my fingers over the minute indentations that formed a crosshatching on the bowl's inner surface. The bottom of the bowl grew thinner and thinner over the years from the blows of the half-moon, mincing knife. Then I put in some leaves and began to chop.

Other rituals stemmed from how we lived. During the summer we didn't use the Jøtul wood stove. Come September we would clean it and the wood box beside it, examine the stove for cracks, and black it. Or in May we would put up screens on the windows and the porch. The house had eighteen windows; the porch had large screens I clamped on that gave us a bug-free place to eat our meals and hang out in the midst of mosquitoes, black flies, and deer flies. Removing the storm windows and hoisting the screens took days, but the work never felt onerous. Summer was near; the cocoon of winter was in the past.

Like all such labor, it had its rhythm—up and down ladders, in and out of the storage shed, washing the fronts and backs of windows. I was never much for the most methodical way to do anything. To be human was to "dub around" in the argot of Maine, as in "What you been up to?" "Oh, dubbin' around." The busy-ness that the society at large made into a virtue (as in, "How are you?" "Busy") seemed pathetic: drowning oneself in the justification of purposefulness. Once upon a time in the Judeo-Christian world, God justified human beings by endowing each person with a soul. Now people strove to justify their existence on their own, as if the energy of mental and physical efforts could provide metaphysical solace: I am busy, therefore I exist. The shorter work week that had been predicted after World War II never happened, for the need to rationalize our unblessed lives through work grew stronger and was still growing. As manias went, it seemed like more Puritan mischief. Rather than let the senses indulge in the textures of life, Puritanism sought to subdue our sensual proclivities in the cult of work. Later (nighttime, weekend, vacation) those proclivities could be indulged to relieve the stress of the work and busy-ness. As one of my Maine neighbors put it, that was "bass ackwards." No wonder Americans swallowed seas of caffeine to keep going. In the woods we did strenuous work most days, but our chores were part of our sustenance. We weren't busy.

The Road Washes Out in Spring

Of the seasonal rituals, the one that stands out most was banking the house. The main part of our house was built on cement piers and open to the weather. When it started to turn cold in November, we put tarpaper around the base of the house to protect it from the elements and to keep out any creatures that might want to spend the winter under our floor. Some years, depending on how motivated we were, we also put old hay around the house for insulation.

We used laths to secure the paper, nailing them directly to the house shingles. You wanted to cut the paper so that it hung down on the ground enough to be secured with a rock. You wanted to overlap the sections so that you could staple them together and an animal couldn't get in. You wanted to slit the bottom of the paper at the house corners with a utility knife so that it wouldn't bunch. Like every task, it had its directives. As we stood in the waning light of the short November afternoon, Janet and I worked together cutting the paper, putting it in place, nailing it, and securing it. Winter was coming; we knew how long winter was. When we stood back and eyed the storm doors, windows, and the black skirt around the house, we felt as ready as we were going to be. Perhaps the banking was no more than a gesture (Stanton did it religiously and laid hemlock and spruce boughs over the hay; Caleb pooh-poohed it), but then most of living seemed a series of gestures. We weren't, after all, living for the benefit of scientific efficiency. We were living to make our feelings palpable, so we could inhabit them literally. The house was our second skin. In buttoning it up for winter a kind of love was at work. The house's endurance was our endurance, too. It was our homestead where, according to the roots of the word "stead," something stood in place and on a place.

We weren't asking for surety or utter protection. We lived day by day. If it was cold, we had to put more wood in the Jøtul. If there was a thaw, we opened the windows and used the cook stove for heat. What we started to feel was how ritual accompanied the weather and seasons. We started to feel the earth's age and our passage on it—the unfathomable length that informed our brevity. Given our devotion to gardening, the holiday ritual that made the most sense to us was Thanksgiving. By that time, the gardens had been put to bed for the winter, although some years we cooked kale leaves and Brussels sprouts that had ice or snow on them. The root cellar held barrels of carrots, beets, and cabbages, along with the potato bin. Opposite the barrels stood the old bookcase that was lined with canning jars full of tomatoes that would form the bases of the soups, sauces, and casseroles that would help carry us through the winter. When we sat down for a meal of baked squash, carrot and raisin salad, lasagna (no turkey for us), and Indian pudding, we were celebrating what we had grown and the earth that sustained us. Before we ate, we bowed our heads and made the traditional Buddhist bow with our hands to our food, a bow of thankfulness and acknowledgment.

We were pilgrims without the capital "P." We respected the good fortune that allowed us to live without the deadly enmities and allegiances that the European settlers of New England had borne. We knew blood had been shed and land stolen; in the next town there had been a massacre of Indians in which eighty men, women, and children along with the Catholic priest who ministered to them were murdered by the English. Such knowing might be the deepest level at which ritual worked—the recognition of how present life is informed by the past and how that past, in its unadorned rawness, wants to be recognized. Through the quirks, intuitions, and misapprehensions of history, the Pilgrim harvest custom was ours. The pine trees that measured ten feet across were gone, but the skunks and raccoons that had so surprised the Pilgrims were here, as were the bluebirds and barred owls, garter snakes and red-spotted newts, sarsaparilla and witch hazel. In that sense their landscape was ours. However remote their spiritual notions were from ours, the simplicity and tenacity of their lives commended themselves to us. Those who stayed were hardy people. They had leapt in as we had in our very different way. Our way was easier but not infinitely so. To feel their blindness was to have compassion for our own. We were no wiser, only further down the road in the American experiment.

We usually went for a walk after the meal. My sister Sherry might be visiting or some friends from the city or my brother-in-law Dave who lived in Vermont. Thanksgiving marked the start of the shortest days. It grew dark early in the thick, enclosing, horizonless woods. The Pilgrims' prayers existed in relation to their fears of the wilderness around them and the wilderness within each human being. Perhaps, despite its titanic optimism, all that the nation they helped found ever wanted to do was to confess those fears.

⁂

Sitting in the rocking chair by the Jøtul wood stove and drinking chamomile tea or Heineken or apple cider, I read about the poets. I wanted to know who these motley presiding spirits were. I wanted their lives to inform mine. It wasn't that I wanted to act as they had. Pound's denunciation of international Jewry or Rimbaud's violence was not what I was looking for. The spectacle of the good, white Wordsworth sinking into the cold, smug lap of Toryism made me queasy—yet I needed to know their unexpurgated stories. I needed some sense of how they went about their lives to make their art, how they moved on, soared, stumbled, fell down, and got up—or didn't get up. I knew that you couldn't be a poet unless flames singed your fingers. Although some went looking for those flames, I also knew that a person didn't have to quest for misfortune and heartache. Mortal life in Somerset County or elsewhere would take care of that. I wasn't interested only in how the poet brought language to bear on the hurt, but also in how the poet grappled with the fact of being a poet.

The metaphor that seized me most deeply and that seemed most apt for the lives of the poets was the subtitle Richard Holmes gave to his remarkable biography of the poet Shelley—*The Pursuit*. Shelley was a perfect example of someone who went where the spirit (and libido) listed and who caused others, such as his first wife, great pain in doing so. You could say he was self-obsessed; you could say he was hypocritical; you could say he was a child-man. I wasn't interested in explanations or judgments. What I needed was the story of someone who believed in the powers of imagination and lived life accordingly—which was Shelley. Inclined as he was to Platonism, it was easy to ridicule him as an impractical fount of poetic blather.

A bit of commonsense might have taught him to swim, for instance (though that would not have saved his life). The intensity, however, with which he pursued poetry (to quote Holmes) as "a sympathetic and human *faculty* [Holmes's italics]—a simple responsiveness to human experience which he called the 'poetry of life'" was genuine. Though poetry went largely unrecognized during these standardized, distracted days, it was not something supplementary. Poetry belonged to us.

The contemporary world with its notions of living one's life according to psychological dicta and shibboleths would have appalled Shelley. In his eyes to be human was to aspire to ideals that were writ large in capital letters—Spirit, Beauty, Art, Love, and Truth. Since we were human, which was to say fallible, we wouldn't reach those ideals, but failure didn't obviate them. On the contrary, like stars they existed to show us that there were realms beyond us that spoke to us and by which we could steer our courses. As we sought to imagine and embody them, they became part of who we were. If, as human beings, we didn't aspire, if we didn't recognize how crucial the pursuit was and the caring and freedom that went with it, our feelings grew dull and monstrous as we fed on satisfactions that did not satisfy. We didn't move to the woods to demonstrate how indifferent we were to materialism; we moved there to see what the life of spirit might be in an undistracted setting. What we sought was a compass. We would have been the first to say that we weren't sure where we were headed; neither did Shelley.

Irony would oppose Shelley and point to his wayfaring feet that usually were dodging bill collectors, but it would not know what to do with his generosity of spirit, for there was no irony there. It was genuine. As Shelley wrote in his famous *A Defence of Poetry*, "The great secret of morals is love, or a going out of our own nature and an identification of ourselves with the beautiful which exists in thought, action, or person, not our own." The terrible blows that idealism has sustained in the historical forms of genocide, world wars, extinction of species, ruination of habitats, and Armageddon weaponry have made us cognoscenti of degradation and stoics of misery. We may be shrewder (though that is doubtful), but we are smaller, too. When, with Aeschylus in mind, Shelley wrote of the titan Prometheus, he wrote of someone who was literally larger than life yet possessed of a vision of what it might mean to be human. Prometheus is defined by his relation to the gods and suffers accordingly. His aspirations must be punished. When one looks at the baffled anti-heroes of modernity, one flinches, for they are human by being less than human. Kafka's Gregor Samsa of *The Metamorphosis* isn't even human. His relationship is not to any god but to the busybody, get-along habits of everyday life. The stuff of myth—metamorphosis—has become absurdity.

The poet's pursuit is for more than the mythic, perfected poem. It is a search for the life that will allow poetry to breathe gladly and fully. I, who never made a to-do about being a poet, admired this search and wondered at it. From my reading it seemed that, unless the poet was willing to turn him or herself into a jester or an ideologue (as happened more than once in the twentieth century), the reply to Shelley's pursuit would be, "Not in this world." Shelley, who was neither jester nor ideologue, rejected that reply. He held that art ministered to life, that the search for form that defined art as an activity was practical Platonism, a phrase that was not a contradiction in terms. Life was not an inferior entity but a passionate search for what was already there. The goodness ("Buddha nature," as the Buddhists would say) was in us. If given a chance, people, like the pines and maples around our house, grew to the light. People wanted to thrive and to love and give love. We humans were, however, febrile creatures, as Shelley bore testimony to in his own life. The response to that fever of feeling wasn't denial. The response was to acknowledge, appreciate, and honor the pursuit as it sought to embody feeling in beautiful forms. Poetry was one ancient way.

Shelley's friend Trelawney remarked on how Shelley was always poring over some Greek text. Shelley revered the forms that were intrinsic to poetry and sought as an artist to make them come to life. A quatrain—to choose one poetic form among many—was, in its own right, something beautiful. It had balance, equipoise, substance, and weight. Yet it could vary substantially in matters such as the length of lines, the sentences it contained, whether it employed end rhymes or not. As a template, it possessed an aura of perfection. It was the poet's vocation to keep that aura alive rather than letting it harden in social usage, as, for instance, when the rhymed quatrain becomes a jingling, narrative box.

This challenge is immense; it isn't hard to see why modernism at times grew impatient with the forms and jettisoned them. Yet a look at a crucial poem such as Ezra Pound's "Hugh Selwyn Mauberley" shows a very modernist poet reinventing a very old form. The end rhymes are there, as in a ballad, but how the quatrain moves, its legerity and self-awareness, are something different. That incredible assertion halfway through the last line of the first stanza—"Wrong from the start"—has the unimpeachable jolt of the form coming to new life. The form does not cancel a human voice; it highlights it.

These forms have come down to the individual poet, and as such, they are gifts that human beings created over long stretches of time. They should be esteemed accordingly. Although esteem can turn into idolatry or pedantry, Shelley, as an artist, sought to balance reverence with active work. For the forms to live, they have to be used. For the forms to be recognized, their absoluteness has to be granted its value. The world of a quatrain is a different world from that of a tercet. If such distinctions aren't recognized and cultivated, then beauty palls. When the quatrain is esteemed, for instance, for its power and acuity, the intensity of the second stanza of Shelley's "The Masque of Anarchy" is possible:

> I met Murder on the way—
> He had a mask like Castlereagh—
> Very smooth he looked, yet grim;
> Seven bloodhounds followed him . . .

We associate revolutionaries with the iconoclasm of sans-culottes, Bolsheviks, and Maoists. As those groups demonstrated to the grief of millions, socialized notions of perfectionism are destructive, intolerant, and coercive. Shelley was a revolutionary in a very different sense. He opposed the swoon of objectivity, the belief that somehow science will do our living for us and all we need do is sign up. He welcomed the findings of science as much as anyone but believed that a human life rejoiced in the presence of the here and now and moved, at the same time, in pursuit of the Good and the Beautiful. The notion that knowledge somehow makes us masters of life would have seemed laughable to him. Our shortcomings, both morally and artistically, remind us of our humanity. That humanity is a river; damming it up changes it into something very different, something more governable but less thrilling. Poets, as Shelley's life and art testified, live for that thrill. Little wonder that the integration of the poet into modern, specialized society has been problematic. The poet is never going to come to the world; the world has to come to the poet. Walt Whitman and Emily Dickinson are still waiting. So is Shelley.

What I felt in Shelley's life and art was a commitment that was complete and real. People often assumed that I moved to the woods to write something called "nature" poems. That was not the case. What the woods gave me was the chance to live a life and write the poems on something like my terms. They were very basic terms—carry the water you bathe in and split the wood that keeps you warm—but they gave me the literal foundation I needed. The Platonist poet was fired by an ardor that had to do with being alive in an actual world of guitars, sunsets, trysts, and tyrants yet feeling the depth of spiritual being that informed that world. Living in the woods allowed for the space, quiet, and solitude to feel that depth so that it became, however provisionally, part of me. There was nothing more inherently "poetic" in my life than in any life. The woods allowed me to grow into my life as the poet I needed to be. The trees chose me as much as I chose them. Had a time machine whisked him forward, I think Shelley—part firebrand, part antiquarian, part dreamer—would have understood. The passionate era that motivated me, the 1960s, would have made sense to him.

Each morning from somewhere in mid-August to somewhere in early June, either Janet or I got up and started a fire in the cook stove. One of us padded downstairs in slippers and pajamas and quickly or not so quickly, depending on the temperature in the house, made sure the damper on the back of the stovetop was open, grabbed a handle to open the circular lid above the front of the firebox, tossed in a few crumpled pages of the *New York Times*—"President Announces"—or *Central Maine Morning Sentinel*—"Hoopsters Vie for Title"—laid some kindling on top of them, struck a match on the stove itself, and lit the papers with it. There was a brief pause as the fire started to take, and then some consideration—more paper, perhaps, or more kindling. Then some sticks of birch or maple went in that weren't too thick and would ignite quickly. There was a light, ardent murmur of air and flame, then a brisk hum as the fire got going. In five to ten minutes, a scintilla of heat started to come off the stove. Whoever else was now up joined fire starter. Each extended cold hands over the stovetop and rubbed them together.

Poets are people who trust metaphor implicitly yet recognize that if pushed too far it loses its potency. The fire that we made each day was the literal fact that was also the metaphorical core of our days in the woods. The solid and massive cast-iron cook stove had a mystical quality as the keeper of the fire. The ancient customs that celebrated and honored the hearth fire as a precious trust made abundant sense. The hearth was honored as the anchor of the domicile, the Latin *domus*, the house, the place where generations gathered and lived. It showed that there was life in the house. It was life.

The flames' shifting shapes figured how protean the fire was. It was tamed but its energy was invincible. It always had to be paid some degree of attention. It was—and I don't think this feeling ever went away—a species of magic. However many fires we started and prodded in the stoves, and surely there were thousands upon thousands of them, each fire was the first fire. I never tired of hearing the cackle and pop of the burning wood. I never tired of staring at the writhe and jump of the flames, of the ever-changing blues and oranges, of the intensity of the coals and then their gradual diminution, their fade into the gray, feathery smudge of ash. I never tired of simply watching one thing—a length of a tree—turn into something else. It was exhilarating and cautionary. Everything could change. Everything would change.

Lighting the fire each day was like renewing a pact with our own lives. We were here in the woods in this house trying to take care of ourselves as best we could. That we lit a fire each day did nothing to diminish our hypnotized stare. What startled me continually was the fire's unintentional beauty. Here was something we made happen that was alive in its own right. Half asleep as I might be in the early January morning, I found myself coming to life with the fire. The student who had burned down the school must have exulted in the power that was fire and by terrible extension what seemed like his own power. By lighting the fire each day, I made obeisance to the fiercest element, the one that seemed to trump the others. A little cycle of finality was enacted daily.

Earth, air, fire, and water were my immediate domain. I could feel how they lived with one another, how the sky gathered water and let it go, how the earth took it in, how the fire we lit heated that water, and how the fire's smoke returned to the sky. Lighting the fire or drawing the water spoke for my role in an essential harmony. Physical need generated the metaphysic of living. Our human minds were prone to straying; the elements, if given a chance, called us back. From that back and forth tug, a centering came. As the story of Prometheus showed, the advent of fire had been an epochal event for humankind. In the dark, cold morning it still was.

When we moved into our house in the woods, we had no idea how long we might stay. We had taken a leap; our heads were spinning with the work we had to do to keep ourselves going, to say nothing of raising children. The wood I had cut in clearing our house site was not near enough to get us through the coming winter. I worked steadily through the fall and winter cutting up dead trees, splitting them, and staying barely ahead. Sometimes I found myself sawing and splitting by a flashlight that I perched on a tree stump—ridiculous, but then we had no backup furnace.

The daily labor focused us on what was immediate. We kept track of time the way most people keep track—via birthdays, New Year's

Eves, summers, our wedding anniversary—but there was a reverie-like quality to our lives. Sitting beside kerosene lights and reading Dickens or Jane Austen or Keats, rising occasionally to throw a log in the stove, we joked about not knowing what century it was. When we looked out the window there were only shadowy trees in the primeval darkness. The little glow inside the house felt very vulnerable.

Our children grew up in that house, eventually leaving it to go to boarding school and then to college. Our lives as they were embodied in the day to day of cooking, tending fires, bringing in wood, pouring water into pots, buckets, tubs, and pitchers were close-knit, and when the children left (and they were no longer children), their absence made the solitude stronger. The house was a home for human voices; we missed theirs deeply. Janet and I still loved where we lived, but it wasn't the same house without them in it. It was more starkly contemplative and lonelier; we were older. We continued to walk and wonder and talk about childhood memories or recipes for butternut squash or righting one of the woodsheds that seemed to be tilting or a story we had read by Chekhov or how there seemed to be more goldfinches around but fewer grosbeaks. As we hiked the abandoned roads and paused to observe an old vireo nest, catkins that carpeted the ground, the scrim of ice that coated a puddle, or pinecones that had fallen the night before in a hard wind, it was hard to imagine another life. Yet we knew we would leave one day.

Buddhists preach non-attachment. It's easy to say but hard to do. Attachment is central to our feelings as human beings. It may be childish, imperious, and grasping, but there it is. A monk's feeling, I would guess, is direct and cosmic. There is nothing to hold onto, and the moment is all there is. Time makes no promises; the mind spins no comforting scripts. Permanence is as much a dream as transience. We weren't monks, but we knew how quickly human efforts are effaced, how in not many years the aspens and pines fill a field, how the woods around us once had been those fields. The scythe I used to keep down whatever sprouted in the open area behind our vegetable garden was not an affectation. The edges of the woods were always moving closer.

The Road Washes Out in Spring

To leave the house was to relinquish a dream that we had brought to life. The house was where we experienced life on earth most fully, where we came to know the sun and rain and stars, the snow and mud and wind. We knew them before, but we didn't know them. We didn't let them into our being the way they entered our being when we lived so simply in the woods. They constituted life on earth, and we were living life on earth. It was uncomplicated—that was what kept us so rapt. It put the inventions and ideologies of humankind into a perspective that refused to warp or bend. We knew some of the work it took to keep a modest household going; we knew how gratifying that work was, how it satisfied us because it was so tangible. We were participators in a world much larger than we were yet one that fit our lives quite seamlessly. We felt we belonged on earth. I have to wonder how many people ever feel that.

The great Polish poet Zbigniew Herbert wrote during the long misery of communism a poem entitled "Report from the Besieged City." It contains these lines: "if the City falls but a single man escapes / he will carry the City within himself on the roads of exile / he will be the City. . . ." We lived in the Country with a capital "C," but Herbert's lines spoke to the importance of inwardness, of how being can bear itself forward while honoring its past. Our lives as we lived them in the woods went by. One day we loaded a truck with our not many possessions and moved to a house in a town thirty or so miles away. When Janet and I looked back at our house as it sat in its clearing, we cried. It had been utterly ours. We could have stayed, but we knew we didn't want to hold on. We never wanted to hold on. We carried the house in the woods within us.

Acknowledgments, continued from page iv

Holt and Company. Copyright 1944, 1951 by Robert Frost. Reprinted by permission of Henry Holt and Company, LLC.

Excerpt from "Gettysburg: July 1, 1863" copyright 2005 by the Estate of Jane Kenyon. Reprinted from *Collected Poems* with the permission of Graywolf Press, Saint Paul, Minnesota.

"Autumn Lines" and excerpt from "High in the Mountains, I Fail to Find the Wise Man" from *Five T'ang Poets*, translated and introduced by David Young, Oberlin College Press, copyright © 1990. Reprinted by permission of the publisher.

Excerpt from "Regarding Chainsaws" from *Collected Shorter Poems 1946–1991* by Hayden Carruth, Copper Canyon Press, copyright 1992. Reprinted by permission of the publisher.

Excerpt from "I Sleep a Lot" by Czeslaw Milosz from *The Collected Poems 1931–1987*, HarperCollins Publishers, copyright © 1988. Reprinted by permission of the publisher.

Excerpt from "Report from the Besieged City" by Zbigniew Herbert from *Report from the Besieged City & Other Poems* by Zbigniew Herbert. Translated with an Introduction & Notes by John Carpenter and Bogdana Carpenter. HarperCollins Publishers, copyright © 1985 by Zbigniew Herbert. Reprinted by permission of the publisher.

Excerpt from *Wise Blood* by Flannery O'Connor, Farrar, Straus and Giroux, copyright 1949, 1952, 1962. Reprinted by permission of the publisher and Harold Matson Co., Inc.

Excerpt from "The Death of the Ball Turret Gunner" by Randall Jarrell from *The Complete Poems* by Randall Jarrell, Farrar, Straus and Giroux, copyright 1968, 1969 and Faber and Faber, Ltd. Reprinted by permission of the publishers.

Excerpt from "Hugh Selwyn Mauberley" by Ezra Pound from *Selected Poems* by Ezra Pound, New Directions Publishing Corporation, copyright 1957. Reprinted by permission of the publisher.

Library of Congress Cataloging-in-Publication Data

Wormser, Baron.
The road washes out in Spring : a poet's memoir
of living off the grid / Baron Wormser.
p. cm.
ISBN-13: 978-1-58465-607-4 (cloth : alk. paper)
ISBN-10: 1-58465-607-7 (cloth : alk. paper)
1. Wormser, Baron. 2. Poets laureate—Maine—Biography. 3. Poets,
American—20th century—Biography. 4. Country life—Maine. I. Title.
PS3573.O693Z46 2006
811'.54—dc22   2006017923